Revie

"The Middle Aged Goddess Playbook is not only a 'must read' but a 'must need'! It is a fantastic quest for any female warrior going into the third stage of a woman's life. Well done Shakti for uplifting my day and for being on my bedside!"

Anaiya Sophia author of Sacred Relationships (Inner Traditions, USA)

"The Middle-Aged Goddess Playbook' is full of spiritual wisdom and practical guidance. The timeliness wisdom in this book will help you find your inner Goddess. It will also connect you to a path that will make your heart sing."

Steve Nobel, author, spiritual coach and founder of Soul Matrix Healing

"Shakti's book, The Middle-Aged Goddess, is a wonderful account of her incredible and remarkable journey! An inspirational, and very moving and informative account of Shakti's experiences (as well as her wonderful sense of humor). I am excited to follow some of the exercises in this playbook – especially having seen how much she has transformed over the last four years since starting to write the book! Shakti has a zest for life, for passion and for sharing everything that she learns that one doesn't see too often. She looks radiant and has certainly found the key to lasting youthfulness. Shakti is an inspiration to so many women (and men) and I am so grateful to this wonderful lady for inspiring me into my own journey of being a Ma Goddess!"

Vicki McKellar, actress and playwright, The Marilyn Conspiracy

The Middle-Aged Goddess Playbook

by

Shakti Kali Kaloczi

Published by
The Endless Bookcase
Available from: www.theendlessbookcase.com

The Endless Bookcase
71 Castle Road, St Albans, Hertfordshire, England UK, AL1 5DQ

ISBN: 978-1-912243-25-9

This book is available in a variety of formats both paper and electronic.

Dedication

One of the best friends I have ever had has died. Rachel was a beautiful soul and she also suffered with depression. She would have so loved this book. Rachel had such a traumatic life from childhood, to having children at a very young age, to losing her mum whilst pregnant aged fifteen. Rachel and I were soul sisters. We met just two years before she died, and I will never forget the joy that this beautiful Goddess bought into my life.

This book is in memory of you, Rachel Long.

1971-2016

Photographer: Antonio Casiero

About the Author

Elizabeth Shakti Kaloczi was born in 1961, the eldest daughter of Hungarian refugee, Ferenc Kaloczi. Aged seven, she was finally allowed the ballet classes she'd dreamed of for many years when her grandmother offered to pay for them. At eleven, her audition to the Royal Academy was cancelled because she had glandular fever a few weeks before the audition. Never quite 'fitting in' Elizabeth dropped out of college until her mother found her a course in Fashion at Leicester Square's College For The Distributive Trades. But the thought of working her way from office junior to senior fashion buyer wasn't appealing. After gaining her diploma she quit her prestigious job in a central London fashion house and continued with a string of jobs, her longest employment was just six months in a local mental hospital, her shortest job was a half day at 'Our Price Records' where Elizabeth simply wanted to see if she could beat the other fifty or so applicants by being offered a job in the very trendy new record store.

From market stalls to selling washing powder made by paraplegics in Sydney, normal 'working life' simply didn't appeal to this young lady. So, she made a vow, never again to work for anyone else.

Her dream was to have a family, and two days before her 21st birthday and only days after her family had emigrated to Australia, she met her first husband, Steve Taylor.

Elizabeth's family returned from Australia with the early eighties recession and Liz returned home with new punk husband in tow and her four-week-old baby. Three years later her second son arrived. But then tragedy struck. Her young husband was diagnosed with cancer aged just twenty-five. Her new-born baby was put on a life support machine, and Liz was widowed five months later, on Mayday 1987.

Steve's funeral was exactly five years to the day that she had met him in Perth on 5th May 1982.

A second marriage, and then a divorce in 1999 and a string of relationships followed. Liz's Post-Traumatic Stress Disorder was disrupting her new-found career as an aerobics teacher. Her second marriage had been a deep soulmate connection, but the relationship died as the desire to live the rock n' roll lifestyle diminished in favour of health and more natural and authentic living.

After her divorce, which was 'gut- wrenching' and heart-breaking, the guilt that her boys had 'lost' a second father caused her deeper anguish. Life was throwing it in faster than this young mum could cope with. She found herself dealing with two hormonal teenage boys and all this took its toll on her health.

Life at times became unbearable. Prayers seemed to help where nothing else could. Liz finally discovered a new way of living. She studied Yoga, Pilates and natural health, she created fit from within, a philosophy for life. Her beloved mother died aged just sixty-five, and Elizabeth was diagnosed with an incurable disease, Ulcerative Colitis. After six years of drug therapy she decided to come off all medication and to heal naturally. This became her number one focus. With grown up boys now in their late twenties, she decided to train teachers in her Pilates studio and travel the world. Not allowing negative thoughts into her mind, she started visualising and creating her dream life. Some of her long-term clients, many who had been loyal for over 20 years, were upset that she was 'leaving them'. However, they eventually realised that in order to continue her teaching, Liz needed to travel. After an invitation to teach in Thailand at an exclusive detox resort it was Liz herself who declared 'How can I teach this stuff unless I live it?!!'

At fifty, she realised that travel was essential to her life's journey, and she ignored the 'you can't afford it' voices in her head, and did it anyway.

In August 2017, after going through a spiritual awakening, Elizabeth Shakti changed her name to Shakti Kali, finally ready to embody the energy of the goddess, allowing everything that she'd previously known to fall away. Time to live the dream, and to encourage other middle-aged women to do the same, to 'find their Shakti' and live with purpose, presence and passion.

Making the Most of This Book

As if reading this book isn't enough, I have a very special gift for you! As a beautiful accompaniment to this book I invite you to join me on my support and mentoring website Riseshakti.com and sign up for your complimentary videos, meditations, health and beauty tips and exercises. I will stand by you all the way, offering support, guidance and love when you most need it. So, before you begin, I suggest that you go to the site and register your name for immediate access.

In true Goddess style there are random paragraphs beginning 'Take your Playbook' where I invite you to do little exercises, practices and journaling. I recommend buying yourself a beautiful journal as well as using the blank pages at the end of this book. You know, for those 'aha' moments when passion and spontaneity give priority over scheduled journaling. Keep the book by your bedside and open at random pages for daily insights once you've read it through. Each reading becoming a subtle reminder of the potent and transformational energies available to you!

Everything I teach comes first-hand and from my own experience. What I share in this book and on the Rise Shakti website is 100% tried and tested. I share my heart with you siStar.

And I love you very much.

For I am another you.

In L'akesh.

Shakti

Contents

Foreword

You are so ready for this exciting journey! (Or you would not be reading this book.)

You are ready, and this is the moment. An evolution is beginning now in which you will feel more powerful, more beautiful, more loved and more cherished than ever before. I am telling you this because I have been on this journey of Self-discovery for many years: the tears, the pain, the drama, loneliness, self-pity, illness, loss, disease, wonderment, sadness, grief, the evolving spirit, the bliss and the joy!

I was never actually drawn to the Goddess faiths such as Paganism, and the negative connotations around witchcraft always left me somewhat intrigued. In my forties I was told by a tarot reader in Glastonbury that I ought to investigate kundalini energy and that I would work with women. That was quite a surprise to say the least. I loved being around men, and although I always connected deeply with other women I certainly had no intention of holding workshops, courses or even writing books for women.

Living my punk lifestyle as a young mum, married to an addict and then later another addict, my life was taken up with dealing with grief, caring for my children and getting out of my head whenever possible. My real fascination in the whole subject has been sparked in recent years. The identification with The Goddess was for me, more natural than a male deity. In witchcraft, a woman can become a High Priestess, equal to that of the male High Priest, or the hedge-witch who tunes in with an altruistic energy and helps others with her herbs and healing remedies. She is not part of any group and works with her own magical intuitive powers. For me ultimately, the relationship with the divine and my quest for spirituality has always been my driver regardless of faith, religion, culture or creed. I've had a keen interest in Tantra, though sadly I've not yet found the truest version anywhere outside of my own intuitive version of integrity and alignment, and I share my experiences and stories in these pages.

I look back and see how much I was sucked into mainstream cultural conditioning. I never really believed in the third dimensional reality and now in my fifties, and with the internet, and of course evolution, we are finally experiencing and witnessing the end of the patriarchal world that we've been so ingrained with on every level and into a new reality- the rise of the Goddess.

Studying and experiencing Shakti energy I am now in full flow, feeling her fulfilling me from the inside out.

"I experience her divinity pulsating through my veins simply by calling her in. Even when things don't feel so good, I honour and thank their presence."

You see, I've learnt some huge lessons on my journey, and I want to share them with you.

It is usual for me now to feel pretty orgasmic every day. I have discovered how to feel joy, inner peace and fulfilment often.

And you can have that too!

This book is all about connecting to your Goddess... to your Shakti wisdom.

What I share in the following pages is a culmination of my colourful life experiences mixed in with ancient wisdoms and teachings plus the practice of working with and cultivating subtle energies, holding heart circles, women's groups and mentoring. And sometimes I lose myself in drama and forget how powerful I am as a human!

Sometimes I get so down, so stuck, and then I come out the other side and remember how true the saying 'this too shall pass' is. In my work I have learnt that it is not just me who is like this, we all are. Life comes along and devastates us. Relationships come and go, children challenge us more than we could ever have imagined, partners let us down and health problems cause worry and pain. But there is always a bigger picture, we get caught up in the stories of our lives and lose sight of what is important to us.

I have studied personal and spiritual development for over 15 years, led heart circles and women's groups, hosted yoga retreats, and had my heart broken too many times to mention. I can guarantee that if you follow the steps in this play book, you will discover a life that has more hope, clarity, presence and love than you ever dreamed possible!

You will discover that life after 40, 50, 60, 70 and 80 can become more meaningful, more beautiful and more magical than at other time in your life.

Oh, beautiful middle-aged Goddess...I am so excited that you're here!

In the old days we were known as the crone. In her positive aspect she is often depicted as a Grandmother, a wise woman, or a midwife. The word Crone is derived from the old word for crown, suggesting that wisdom emanates from the head like a halo. Her own child bearing days are past; she is the wisdom keeper, seer and healer and midwife, whose knowledge is sought out to guide others during life's hardships and transitions.

Unfortunately, in the Middle Ages the church feared these women because they were held in such high esteem within their communities. Many of them were killed during the Inquisition and the wise woman of old was relegated to the Wicked Witch and Hag archetype of our fairy tales. This is a corruption of the original meaning of the words, witch and hag which respectively derived from the word wit, denoting wisdom and hagio meaning holy. Can you believe that? Wise and holy changed to witch and hag!

Today as more women live longer and take more prominent roles within society the tide is starting to turn as we start to reclaim our power.

This book is for you.

This is a book to give to your sisters, your mothers, grandmothers and daughters. This book could be the start to a healthier, happier and more deeply nourishing and enjoyable future.

It is our time.

I bow to you, siStar.

Introduction

Have you ever wondered what your life might look like if you'd ignored everyone else's idea of what you were capable of, and followed your heart 100%? Have you had the feeling that perhaps you spent your whole life giving to others and forgot who YOU really are? Did you marry young for fear of being 'left on the shelf' (as I did), been through a divorce, felt lonely, un-lovable, had trouble earning a good living, found success in business but not in love, struggled with health issues? Felt too fat, too thin, too tall, too short, lacking in confidence, issues from the past, worries for the future?

If you've said 'yes' to any of that then this book is for you. You are going to be catapulted into the realms of the magnificent unknown, where I shall guide you through a series of exercises and thought-provoking ideas which I know will change the way in which you view middle-age forever!

And I need to add something here. Although this book has been written for the 'middle-aged' woman (whatever that might mean) I have scores of women (and men) of all ages waiting to get their hands on my book!

This is a fun, practical, real guide to enhancing your life to bring you more joy, peace, sexiness, health and abundance!

So, let's start at the beginning.

I believe that relationship is the key to everything, to all universal truths, to success, to love, to life itself.

And the most important relationship that you will ever have is the relationship with your higher self, the divine light, Mother Earth, God, Goddess, universal energy, call it what you will. This has nothing to do with religion. In fact, the truths in this play book are woven into many of the religions, because there is only one truth. Interpreted in many ways, by man, where power and control may dilute the original essence of the message.

We are here, you and I, to celebrate our wholeness, our divine, our Goddess within.

This is the energy that shall heal you from your past and carry you to your future. The light that shines within, without, above and below. Inside of you and outside of you.

But enough of my spiritual fluffy stuff,

This book is a practical guide to get in touch with, and meet, the love of your life.

YOU.

You can have the best year of your life ***this year***

You can have the best body of your life ***this year***

You can have inner beauty and peace ***right now***

You can change your life

Today.

At 15, I told my father excitedly about a book on the subject of 'How to be successful and earn lots of money!'

Instead of showing any interest or being excited about my passion he yelled at me 'Blah, American rubbish! Do not believe a word of it!' And so, I never mentioned it nor thought about such an idea again.

Please do not put limits on me

Allow me to be my Divine Self

Do not ask me to believe the way you do

And I will not ask you to believe the way I do.

Do not put limits on me.

Let me shine

Let me dance.

Let me love.

Rachel and Me

Photographer: Antonio Casiero

Part 1

Chapter 1
What is a Goddess?

Goddess lives in every woman. She is the part of you that is beautiful, gorgeous, magnificent, awesome, whole, and a powerful magnet for love, life, and self-expression! She is sexy, lovable, funny and super amazing!

She is a woman who is in the process of learning how to accept herself and love herself on all levels. Mind, body and spirit. She experiences more joy, peace, creativity and abundance as she begins to awaken....

But what happened to that divine feminine Shakti spirit within you?

Where did she go? And how can you reclaim her? I am so excruciatingly saddened to see friends whom I've known for many decades buy into an idea that life 'goes downhill' after 50, with a loss of sexual appetite, and an idea that 'well this is my lot.' And yet I have friends who are in their eighties and have become ageless.

It is our conditioning since childhood to put the needs of others ahead of ourselves. It is not your fault that you were taught to put others first, and as women we have forgotten what real nourishment truly means. We give away our power in so many ways and then wonder why we are so depleted, depressed, fragile and empty.

In our earliest history the reigning deity was the Goddess. She was manifest in the moon, the stars, the flowing rivers, the morning dew, and the fertile earth. She represented the natural cycles of life.

When we arrive at that 'certain age' in the flow of the menopausal and postmenopausal energy, we start to tap into something quite ancient, something innate to all women.

When the Goddess in you arrives at this phase of life she becomes the one others turn to for counsel and comfort.

We have transformed into The Goddess of Wisdom!

Once we've reached fifty our archetypal energies are ready to become expressed and manifest. You are now ready divine, beautiful Goddess - not simply to transform from somebody to somebody else, no, you are ready to *become* the woman that you *always* knew you were. These energies that are going to be aroused in you are awaiting your attention. If you do not allow these natural energies to be expressed and cherished, then you will almost certainly go down the road of old age that is depicted in the old way that was born out of patriarchy and Christianity. We were seen as 'dressing too young' and 'mutton dressed as lamb'. In the past it has been a crime to 'grow old disgracefully.'

SISTARS……. we are SO powerful!

Why do you think we were repressed and put down as second-class citizens?

It is finally time to realise that you are here to light up the world!

When we awaken to the wise woman within who we may have lost through controlling or abusive relationships, running our own businesses or being a career woman and raising our children, we begin to open up to a new potential for a very beautiful, juicy and rewarding experience.

You'll begin to feel liberated, blissed out and more comfortable in your skin than ever before because you'll become who you were meant to be... your real self. The true, authentic expression of your soul. She was always in there, and now is the time to unleash her.

Just writing those words I get a tingle in my yoni!

You are so much more powerful than you could even begin to imagine!

Because we live in such a left brained masculine world of goals, formulas, lists, control, technology and science, the divine feminine spirit has become lost - and many of us have forgotten she even exists. Our feminine qualities of receptiveness, gentleness, nurturing and intuition have not been cultivated or nurtured and we now find ourselves lost in a world of science, deadlines and numbness to our majestic femininity. Masculine power is about control, but feminine power creates more flow, intuition and magic.

Take in a deep breath.

Make yourself a cuppa.

This book will show you how to reconnect with your Goddess, your divine feminine. And from that place your life will take on a new meaning and a deeper and richer experience. You will start to manifest that which your heart desires more effortlessly and you'll become a magnet for love and abundance!

The warrior woman must awaken to her strengths with love, power and dignity.

It does not mean that we control from a masculine perspective, but with a gentle yet powerful inner strength.

I see too many women from all cultures who have taken on too much Shiva (masculine) energy. At an entrepreneurial women's group recently, I was taken aback by how many women were depleted and exhausted. Add to this a poor diet, lack of sleep and exercise and you have a recipe for disaster.

"What was I doing at an entrepreneurial meeting in London?" you might ask. Well I had read about the speaker and had made a pact with myself to get out more! And what I learnt was nothing to do with being an entrepreneurial woman. I learnt how down-trodden and depleted these beautiful souls were on every level. They were literally striving for success in the masculine way and it wasn't working. They were sick and tired of being sick and tired. And the remedy was to try and push for more. More clients, more targets, more sleepless nights, more money.

In truly loving yourself there is magnificent strength which will radiate from every cell of your being.

Have you forgotten what makes you feel truly alive dearest one?

What turns you on? Can you allow yourself, just for a short while, to let go of all your limiting beliefs about yourself and open up to the possibility that you are the creator of your life? That you are powerful *beyond measure*? That the Goddess within is yearning to be set free? Do you feel tired, so tired of limiting beliefs preventing you from living your most magnificent life? How honest can you be with yourself? What is holding you back? Can you begin to take baby steps towards where you want to go and who you want to be?

As George Bernard Shaw once said, *"Life isn't about finding yourself. it's about creating yourself."* Therefore, the process of manifesting from the heart is ultimately a process where you become a powerful, conscious creator, so that you can give birth to a whole new version of yourself

Since tuning in to this energy I now feel orgasmic every single day (more on that later!)

What is your life all about? What makes your heart sing? What do you love doing? What are you good at? What are your special qualities? How do you like to feel? What excites you, turns you on, gets your juices flowing?

Have you forgotten? Did you ever know?

What do you feel you could share with the world, not just those around you but the *whole* world? You think I'm kidding? You think you have nothing to share? Did you know that your soul chose to come here to experience joy? And that joy can be felt most when you are aligned with your highest passion, your highest truths. What makes you *excited*? Did you know that *joy* is your birth-right?

I asked a class yesterday morning to close their eyes and think of something that they wanted to have finished in the next 3 months. I was very surprised that virtually no one could not think of *one* thing. But you see in life, we are always either growing or dying. You cannot stay the same. Nothing stays the same, it will only become stagnant. You may see it (or feel it) as your 'comfort zone'. But comfort zones are hiding places where boredom and frustration sets in. In each moment you are either moving towards your goal (feeling good) or moving away (not feeling good). It is human nature to want to move towards something.

However, sometimes feeling pain can be moving you in the right direction too. This is why *feeling pain can actually be a blissful experience*. Joseph Campbell, the brilliant scholar who documented how people across all cultures and all times are essentially living by common mythologies, is probably most famous for his advice to '*follow your bliss*' but he had to add a clarification because some people took this to mean that they should forgo anything that was unpleasant or distasteful.

But what Campbell believed was that people should find the path in life that fuels their spirit, that speaks to them on the deepest level. But he also said that if your path is just fun and excitement then you are on the wrong path, because 'sometimes pain is bliss'.

An Earl Nightingale story by Denis Waitley, 'The psychology of winning' talks about developing adaptability to the stresses of life and seeing them as normal. Earl Nightingale tells of his visit with his son recently to the Great Barrier Reef which stretches nearly 1800 miles from New Guinea to Australia.

Noticing that the coral polyps on the inside of the reef, where the sea was tranquil and quiet in the lagoon, appeared pale and lifeless... while the coral on the outside of the reef, subject to the surge of the tide and power of the waves, were bright and vibrant with splendid colours and flowing growth...

Earl Nightingale asked why this was so. 'It's very simple,' came the reply, 'the coral on the lagoon-side dies rapidly with no challenge for growth and survival... while the coral facing the surge and power of the open sea, thrives and multiplies because it is challenged and tested every day. And so, it is with every living organism on earth.'

How about you?

Are you so busy trying to make everything appear perfect that you're missing the beauty of the challenging times?

Look at what's happening in America right now. Many are asking 'why are all these women protesting about Trump?' Well if you didn't yet feel it, the awakened Goddess can feel intuitively in her womb when something isn't flowing. SiStars across the globe - and a newly emerging brotherhood too- are rebelling because of a deep knowing that what's happening in our world is not how we want our world to be. And on some level too we also know that it's the shadow playing out. (More on shadows later)

If you go deep within, you will finally stop believing in and supporting this religion of government because it really has never been about any one politician. You cannot "vote for change"

Change is happening now. We are moving into the age of Aquarius. The last thousand years has been all about change. Goddesses in the making, we are on the path towards a true shift and evolution of consciousness.

Life is an ebb and flow like the ocean. There will be 'good' and 'bad' experiences. We cannot say 'no' to what appears to be 'bad' because shit happens! You know that, right? I bet you've had more than your fair share.

I certainly have. But you know what? I decided to use my experiences and transform them into something good. I believed that my experiences had happened for a reason. That my soul had chosen this path, and that whatever came my way, I would find the strength to continue. I started to experience much deeper happiness, inner peace and joy.

And oftentimes I hurt too.

I want to share my story with you because it's been one hell of a journey ....

Say 'YES ' to it all!

Goddess........

I Love You!

Chapter 2
My Story

Sadness does not arise to be healed

It arises to be heard

It arises to be held

In the loving arms of awareness

In April 2015 I walked away from a 3-day Tantra beginner course held in London. The course came highly recommended by a male friend who teaches Tantra. I was dancing vibrantly and full of life to the morning practice, feeling fully embodied and alive. We then started to practice the ancient ritual of shaking. During this time, we were invited to let out any sound/noise from our vocal chords. Some people started making horrific noises. These noises triggered a direct and immediate response to my nervous system like a siren, and within minutes took me right into my nightmare of 29 years earlier. I was taken back to the darkest days of my life, as if in a trance, to the feeling of being trapped in hell and not being able to express how I felt because the trauma was way to enormous for that.

It was as if my emotional body wanted to grieve so hard, and yet my mind could not accommodate the enormity of my devastation. At 25 I had the family I'd dreamed of. A beautiful 3-year-old boy and a 2-month-old baby. I hadn't recovered yet from the huge amount of blood I'd lost after giving birth, and my beloved mother cared for me so well, cooking me red meat and making me eat greens, which were not at that time one of my staples!

This birth had really taken it out of me, especially as I'd had to cope with my young husband's gambling addiction. I was regularly scouring the pubs in our town (especially on payday) because often I would have no housekeeping after Steve had spent his entire week's wages on one-armed bandit machines. On a few occasions I was so desperate for money to feed my babies that I stole a tin of baked beans from a supermarket so that we could have a meal.

The stress of living hand-to-mouth was exhausting enough without being heavily pregnant. I was so beaten up emotionally that I chain-smoked throughout my pregnancy. I was an addict too, to tobacco, as my only way of blocking out the pain in my life. I was constantly lied to, because, as anyone knows who lives with an addict, it comes with the territory.

Being 25 was not fun. So, when my 7-week-old son was rushed into hospital with the worst case of pneumonia ever seen in a baby, my husband was collapsed on our living room floor with severe back pain. I will never forget the night Steve and I were told that Matthew had a 50/50 chance of survival. Steve managed to make it to the hospital with me and we spent the night praying in the parents' room. That night, New Year's Eve 1986 was the worst night of my life.

The prayers I said that night were the hardest, most heartfelt, emotionally charged imaginable. And God and the angels responded by saving my baby.

Although New Year's Eve had been seriously life-threatening, the weeks that followed were traumatic beyond belief.

I was so determined to keep my breast milk that whilst my baby was attached to life-saving drips, I was either by his side or wandering down the long, cold and dark corridors of the old Victorian hospital in the middle of the night, where I would attach myself to a large machine which would extract my milk so that my baby could have my breast milk once he had recovered.

Those were some of my darkest hours.

Matthew was still extremely sick, but the worst was over. The tubes in his mouth became less painful to see but my world had been rocked beyond anything I could have ever imagined. And then the bombshell. Five doctors from our surgery had seen Steve, who was now permanently lying on the lounge floor as his back pain was so intense that he couldn't bare the movement of the bed. He had lost 3 stone. And all that the damned Doctors could come up with was to 'stay lying down on the floor because you have sciatica!'

I have so many heart wrenching stories from this period, with my GP acting inhumanely at times. After weeks and weeks of Steve being in acute pain, he wasn't even so much as offered a blood test. With much difficulty I managed to get a new GP. Matthew came home from hospital after being on the children's ward for a month. Exactly ten minutes after I arrived home with my baby in my arms I got a phone call with the news that was to change my life forever.

Steve was diagnosed with a serious blood abnormality. I pleaded with the doctor to tell me what this meant. He declined to confirm anything much to my alarm. I begged. 'Please tell me, what is the worst-case scenario?'

The doctor told me that nothing was absolute, but that the worst thing it could be was Leukaemia. I felt sick to the stomach. I had just spent nearly a whole damned year feeling sick to the stomach, and in particular the last month, when my precious new baby had nearly lost his fight for life.

The next day was a Sunday. Steve was due to be seen for an appointment on the Monday morning. But on the Sunday, he began to bleed, and he was taken into hospital where he was put onto a drip.

On the Monday I had an appointment with the specialist who told me that my husband had non-Hodgkin's Lymphoma.

Steve began a tough course of chemotherapy, and Matthew returned to hospital with further chest complications.

Adam my 3-year-old, was passed around family and friends, I lived at the hospital spending time in Steve's isolation room wearing a mask, and then would go downstairs to the children's' ward to be with Matthew.

I lived like this for about 5 months. Until I heard the news that tore me apart. That closed me down. That left me paralyzed, unable to eat, unable to think, unable to function.

The day that the specialist told me that Steve had 2 weeks to live, shattered all the false hopes and dreams that I'd had about our life together as a happy family.

The day I took my babies into the hospital to say goodbye to their daddy was the hardest thing I've ever had to do in my life. The nurses were beside themselves, and many of them could not contain their grief. For me, for my boys, and for themselves. I wanted to die too but my boys needed me. Everyone said to me 'You are strong,' and 'God only gives you what you can handle'. I hated that! I didn't feel strong and I didn't feel able to cope.

"Life will break you. Nobody can protect you from that, and living alone won't either, for solitude will also break you with its yearning. You have to love. You have to feel. It is the reason you are here on earth. You are here to risk your heart. You are here to be swallowed up. And when it happens that you are broken, or betrayed, or left, or hurt, or death brushes near, let yourself sit by an apple tree and listen to the apples falling all around you in heaps, wasting their sweetness. Tell yourself you tasted as many as you could."

~ Louise Erdrich

I met my second husband soon after, and there was an instant attraction. I was desperate to find someone to save me, and Paul became my prince in shining armour - um, I mean in leather trousers....

Paul was 23 and I was 26 and we'd both been through trauma. The first time my son Adam met Paul, on around our third date, Paul pushed Adam on a swing in the pub's garden and Adam asked, 'are you going to be my new daddy?'

I fell madly in love with Paul, and even though I would often awake in the night sobbing in disbelief about what had happened to Steve, I knew deep down that Paul was 'the one'. We drank a lot, smoked a lot, fought a lot and had sex a lot.

I loved our crazy banter, and I loved to get out of my head on marijuana. The day I married Paul was the happiest day of my life. After nearly twelve years, drink became my reason for our breakup. We had many challenges, and in particular my eldest son was becoming unbearable to live with at home. It was like living in a mad house.

Adam would smash objects around the home, I remember not long before Paul walked out for good that I had to endure dinner plates being thrown across the conservatory. To this day, I still love Paul and I know that he loves me. Perhaps in another lifetime we can be together again.

It was soon after Paul left that I discovered that Adam had been severely bullied at school. I had a call from the school asking me to take him to a child psychologist because he'd just thrown a table across the classroom. I told them that although Adam was emotional it was not in his nature to throw tables around. I simply couldn't believe that my son was reacting in this way. I collected him from school and took him for lunch where he broke down and confessed that he'd kept his secret for 5 years. He'd been severely traumatised by two boys at school for the entirety of his secondary school experience. He'd been beaten, locked in cupboards, had dog excrement thrown at him - and was frightened of the threats of this gang of boys, many of whom didn't even attend my boy's school. Poor Adam, although popular at school, feared the threat of a knife gang, and didn't want any teachers to be told.

So not only did I have to deal with Paul's departure and subsequent divorce, but now my fifteen-year-old son, about to take his GCSE exams, was my priority. The amount of energy it took to organise his life at that time took its toll, and again I became weighed down with PSTD and total adrenal burnout.

Years later, the mother of the bully 'gang leader' attended my aerobics classes. She was so nice and sweet, but I wanted to tell her 'your son ruined my boy's childhood!'

Of course, I didn't tell her because Adam asked me not to. But the stress caused in my house during those years was the reason that Paul gave for leaving.

Take your Playbook

What is Your story? Take your time to really get into the feelings and memories of how it was for you. Give yourself the gift of time, just a couple of hours. Even better, can you take a weekend getaway just for the purpose of this Playbook? I remember the very first time I ever went away for a 'me time' weekend. I was in my early 40's. My partner at the time, from a five-year relationship after Paul, actually suggested it. I always wondered if he said it just because he would have a few days without my 'puppy-like' behaviour as he called it. I was going through another episode of PTSD, and couldn't manage to walk for more than 5 minutes without being exhausted. (This was me at my best during such an episode, many times I would be bed-ridden)

My few days in Glastonbury, England were some of my very first trips away alone and I remember feeling somewhat awkward and yet privileged that I could be given the space to 'find myself'.

See if you can literally 'lose yourself' in this task. Notice how you feel once you've written everything that you can.

It's amazing how by giving yourself time and space to write down your own story, that emotions can be felt and released. If it gets uncomfortable at any time just simply breathe more deeply. Know that you are safe and loved. We've endured a lot haven't we sister?

Allow the part of you that wants to feel, to be given some loving space. Write it all down in your Playbook. Take your time to visit some feelings. This is the start of your healing, beautiful Goddess.

Chapter 3
The Power of Belief

The Law of attraction is at work all the time, whether we are aware of it or not. You may have read *The Secret,* but my recommendation would be that you spend some time listening to Abraham Hicks on YouTube. No one knows the law of attraction like Abraham.

Your words and thoughts have great meaning and a very high vibration. And like everything else in the universe, the energy they generate cannot ever dissipate into the cosmos. It must go somewhere; it must always exist after you have created it. Your words and thoughts will always attract more energy and create your reality.

Science has proven this too, and NLP has also become very popular. I think of NLP as the 'thinking man's' yoga.' The scientific process of Neuro Linguistic Programming (NLP) explains how the mind processes information, transforms it to desire through language, and creates a new reality.

One of the founding principles of NLP separates fact from perception, and your power to create reality. Bandler and Grinder drew from the work of famed philosopher and scientist Alfred Korzybski. Korzybski developed a theory that no person has direct knowledge of reality or truth.

Everything we believe, feel, and think comes from our own perceptions based on our specific set of experiences. As Korzybski put it: "The map is not the territory." The reality you use to map your life is different from your neighbour's reality, or your ancestor's reality. Your truth is true to you because you have generated it from your own life!

And that means you have the power to create a NEW reality based on your new set of experiences. When you control your experiences and create new thoughts, these thoughts travel beyond you, generating an energy that expands to the heavens and attracts like energy back to you.

Now don't get me wrong, I truly love what NLP stands for and what it does for people. It's scientific. And you know what, us Goddesses don't mind a little science now and again, but we much prefer to work with the natural laws where there is no 'need' for the head (mind) to get over complicated. To me, science is just a documented research and proof that something is 'true'.

However, the natural laws are natural phenomena. Like the law of gravity. I don't need to do scientific research to 'prove' the law of gravity. And so, it is with the law of attraction (LOA)). It's quite subtle and deeply profound and it also requires practice just like anything else that you want to develop.

You are a Thinking, Speaking Magnet. So, what does NLP have to do with the Law of Attraction? In short, everything.

When you tell the Universe what you want, and repeat your affirmations to yourself every day, your meaningful words will create change because they have come from your subconscious.

Your subconscious has a high magnetic vibration and connects to the Universe in a very powerful way. Words that originate from this deeper structure in your subconscious have the power to generate change and action. Trust yourself and your desires, and let your language come from this place of knowing. You will be amazed at how much quicker your dreams manifest when you speak them from your subconscious. It's really all about being present and conscious.

"I am money."

"I receive wealth."

"I receive love."

These are not merely words on the surface; they are meaningful vibrations from your subconscious.

Even the words you speak on a regular basis during your daily life should come from this deeper place where you can use your language to be positive and manifest your desires. When you know yourself well, and you have internalised your intentions, it won't even be something you have to think about. You will naturally speak from this deeper aspect of yourself, because you will be constantly tapped into it.

This means you can use your thoughts to create a new reality, and align your words with your desires.

We're all talking about a new paradigm, a paradigm shift, and about how we are moving from a masculine, patriarchal world into the feminine heart centred caring new world. Well beautiful, it ain't gonna happen unless you, yes YOU start practicing working daily on your thoughts, words, deeds and actions. You can programme your mind to generate exactly what you want to receive. But, you've got to believe it. This is where, so many people fail. Belief is *everything.*

Let's say you want to find the love of your life. So far, you have meditated every day on the qualities you want your future lover to have, and you can experience yourself with your mate in your visualisations. But nothing has happened yet, and you fear being alone for the rest of your life. You can call upon the law of attraction (some will call this NLP) to eliminate the fear in your mind by removing "aloneness" from your perception entirely.

Instead, you allow yourself to dwell only on "love." This is your only true thought. Then you align your language with your dream. In your deepest subconscious, you believe that your love is waiting for you, searching for you, and will be revealed to you at the perfect time.

This deep belief becomes the basis for every word you speak. You speak love, hope, and positivity. No matter what others around you are saying, your words are overflowing with love, and you believe you will receive it.

In this way, your mind has created a new life of love for you, and all your decisions and behaviours will be programmed to receive this love when it comes your way. But it's all very well reading this, I'm going to give you an example of how it works.

So, you say to yourself *'where is my soulmate*?'

By asking the question, the vibration that you're putting out to the world is 'I am lacking'

The universe therefore, will give you more lack, like a huge magnet in the sky!

So, try saying 'My heart is now open to receive the love of my soulmate'

Better...... although it's still kind of relying on another to make you feel .... (fill in the words).

Try saying to yourself 'I am feeling love. Take yourself on a date, find the feelings.... Find the words... imagine how it would feel to be on the date with your soulmate, what words come to mind?

Soothed, loved, relaxed, happy, excited, dreamy.

What other words can you think of? Even writing these words down gives a sense of peace and tranquillity in my core.

I am in Bali right now, and at the beach. I have been thinking about these wonderful feelings, and even imagining my soulmate walking with me hand in hand along the beach. Not so much a longing, more an actual believing that he's already here, with me! And yesterday I was sitting in a quiet remote cafe on the computer here where I am writing this book, and a gorgeous hunky 6ft 5 surfer and I started chatting. The cafe is usually empty, and it turned out that he never usually eats in here. It was his last day in Bali, but we spent a lovely time together. He showed me that when my heart is open to receive, that little miracles can happen, as if by chance.

But I say, never by chance.

Always on purpose.

You are constantly creating your reality, beautiful......

OK, let's keep it simple (why would we want to complicate things?) If I were to make a chocolate cake and in it I knew that chocolate was required, it is possible that without a recipe I might not put enough chocolate and too much butter and honey. It becomes gooey ad thick. (Mmmmmm.... perhaps this is not such a great analogy as I think this sounds rather delish!!!)

Ok, so my point is, if we are so goal driven and focussed, without the *Law of Attraction,* we may end up with our chosen outcome, but possibly not the very *feeling* that we were hoping for.

Let me give you an example.

Some years back, I put out to the universe that I wanted to attract a boyfriend. I also really wanted to get my hands on a 'shabby chic' dressing table which I'd seen in a shop window in my home town of St Albans. But it was way too expensive to even consider buying.

I did the work and low and behold within a matter of weeks I had the sexy handsome boyfriend *and* I found an exact replica (in fact there were 2) of the dressing table that I wanted in our local second-hand furniture shop for £60!

What you put your attention to grows.

However, after the initial excitement, passion and butterflies (we kissed a lot, we danced to Mariah Carey in my living room for hours, I really fancied my hot Turkish Cypriot ex footballer/basket player champion!), the relationship proved difficult, emotional and challenging. And the dressing table? Well, it did make me happy, until further along my journey 3 years later when I gave the piece of furniture to my niece as I wanted to let go of all my material goods and seek a simpler life.

My point is, I attracted exactly what I had asked for. But I was filling a need inside of me, trying to fix me from the outside.

I never really found a *real* honest feeling of depth to my happiness. I was elated, joyful, *feeling sexy* and wanted, but I was not *honest with myself.*

These manifestations were merely like Elastoplast fixing a broken fingernail. They were never going to heal nor last.

Do I believe that I needed these experiences? Yes, and this for me, is the magic of maturity, I've had so many opportunities to learn. This is how we grow, *this is what life is all about!*

So, as this law is so important, I'm going to repeat what I've already said!

Whatever you can believe you can achieve.

This was my mantra for many, many years. I drove it deep into my subconscious mind.

Most people spend their time putting their attention on what they lack instead of what they choose to create, so they get more lack. This is where I think that so many of us get caught up in the 'hows, whys and where's.

One thing you must know.

The universe is constantly responding to your thoughts-

Both positive and negative. You really do not have to know how why or where. The universe is like a massive computer.

Whatever you put into your mind must show up sooner or later. It's law.

Let's say for example that you want to start a new business. Any thoughts that you're thinking such as 'I don't think I'm capable of running my own business' will start to attract further negative thoughts (this is the law of attraction in action). It's like you're banging a drum, and the more of what you're thinking, the louder the drum gets.

We start to then believe our thoughts and the law of attraction literally attracts those situations, people and experiences that back up our belief. Now, if you were to notice what you were thinking, and changed the thought to 'I reckon I could do this...' notice the feeling that comes up. If it's not a good feeling begin to think of all the ways that you would feel as if you've already started to run your own successful business. Enjoy the feelings because these feelings will attract more of the same.

It's soooo cool!

If you're still struggling with finding the feeling, then this is what you need to do:

Try to remember a time in your life when you felt capable. Perhaps it was when your dad asked you to help him do something, or your teacher gave you a pat on the back for some project you'd taken your time over. Take yourself back to that time and enjoying the feelings of feeling capable (of course, you can use any feeling that you choose, if you're looking for more happiness start to remember a time in your life when you felt happy). Bathe in them! Those feelings will start to attract better feelings.

On a side note, I always remember my ex, who studied NLP with Richard Bandler, asking a group in a workshop to remember a time in their life when they felt really happy. One lady started to cry. When my ex asked what the matter was, she sobbed 'I've never felt happy in my life, ever!'

So, I always tell my clients, feeling 'happy' can literally be having an early morning cup of tea, listening to the birds singing, or having a chat with your friend. Anything to find that better feeling is going to attract better feelings, It's law.

I work with this law daily- and it can literally jump me from feeling lousy and pathetic (yes, even me my dear, more than you could begin to know) and into the feeling that I'm reaching for the stars.

Now, dream away, beautiful Goddess...

Creative Visualisation

Your purpose is not in what you do, it's in who you are.

Visualising is essential in this Goddess game. You gotta be really good at allowing yourself to daydream, to 'go there' to master the feeling, the look, the vibe of your wildest dreams.

The spiritual teacher, Esther Hicks said:

"Seventeen seconds of focused, pleasurable visualisation is stronger than 2000 hours of working to obtain a goal."

This works for me! The feminine really doesn't need all this goal setting. We are all masculine and feminine energies, but for those of us identified with a feminine body we must remember that we have been under the influence of male leaders for millennia. How many 'Goddess' figures have you been inspired by, ruled by, devoted to? Religious and spiritual figures (Jesus, Buddha etc), presidents, leaders, have generally all been men. And the masculine is the structure, stillness, solid.

The Goddess is *not* goal oriented, but the question is, 'what are my dreams, passions and desires?'

I first came across *creative visualisation* in the early '90's after discovering a book of that title by Shakti Gawain. I began to follow the instructions in the book and couldn't believe what was possible simply by the power of visualising! You see most people only set goals at the conscious level — which is only around less than 5% of our potential resources.

Cutting-edge research from Dr. Bruce Lipton at Stanford University Medical Centre, affirms that it is our subconscious mind that is in control of how much happiness, success, love and abundance that we allow into our lives. Dr Lipton explains that *"most people don't even acknowledge that their subconscious mind is at* play *when the fact is it is a million times more powerful that the conscious mind, and that we operate 95 to 99 percent of our lives from subconscious programmes."*

And your subconscious mind has been programmed with a blueprint that contains limits for (among other things) how happy you can be, how much money you'll make, what your relationships can be like, what type of vacations you'll take, how fit you can become, what kind of car you'll drive...

So, it is our job to identify all those beliefs that have been ingrained into our deepest core - and to set ourselves free from limiting beliefs.

Take your Playbook

I want you to imagine what your perfect life would look like.

Don't limit yourself. Write down what you're doing, whom you are with, where you are, how you feel, what you're wearing. Breathe more deeply, and allow yourself to really go there. What does your day look like, every day? How do you feel?

I want you to stop what you're doing right now!

Put down this book, move away from your laptop and close your eyes.

Try to visualise yourself really being the person that you might've wanted to be.

The woman that you are deep inside the wrappings of fear, sadness, judgement and doubt. The real you waiting to get out and reveal herself to the world.

Now write down at least 10 things that you want. And from the list choose 3 things that you most would like to pursue. As an example, my top 3 would be:

1/ I make the time to enjoy a green juice every morning because my health is important to me.

2/ I am going to write a book about everything I have learnt on my journey so far.

3/ I am going to create an exciting and informative YouTube channel.

Other ideas could include painting old furniture and selling it, starting up an online business, organising a weight loss meetup group locally, helping at the local hospice, fundraising events for local charities, studying a degree, learning to swim, the list is endless!

Please know that if you have always been very shy and you want to be confident, this can be a lot for the brain to take in. A certain amount of fear or even chaos may prelude some big changes, especially as we start to change long term held beliefs about who we are. At this point I absolutely have to tell you about my niece Kylie.

Kylie was an extremely shy little girl. I was so excited to have a niece, especially as I already had a son and was about to have my second son. I was always a girlie girl who loved baby dolls and baby clothes. When Kylie was a toddler she was painfully shy. She would hide behind her mum and go to great efforts not to be noticed. Throughout her school years she struggled to really have a voice.

A few years ago Kylie joined my very first heart circle, and something that I would refer to as pure magic happened. In heart circles we allow pure presence. We notice what emotions are alive in us and allow them to sit with us.

On the first heart circle Kylie openly told the group how shy she had been as a schoolgirl. Her voice shook, and her energy was frail. I was quite shocked because this was not the Kylie that I experienced any longer. But her fear of speaking in public was very present as she told the group of her painful shyness throughout her school years.

At the end of the session Kylie left abruptly, and told me afterwards that she had cried out her eyes (and heart) all the way home. She realised that she was continually living a lie as a hairdresser, engaging in small talk with clients and never really being her true self.

At the next meeting Kylie was a changed woman. She spoke with clarity and confidence. She had experienced an epiphany, a lightbulb moment. Kylie realised that every time she was bubbly, confident and connected she would say to people 'this is not the real me! The real me is very shy and reserved.' Kylie believed this to be true, because she had heard these words repeated so many times as a child that they had become ingrained as a belief. Talk about a changed woman!

Watching this powerful transformation before my very own eyes with my beautiful niece, who now is blossoming into the most awakened thirty-year-old woman imaginable, is beyond what I could have believed. The change in Kylie was astounding!

Magic is happening in front of my eyes more and more, everyday magic happens. But, dear Goddess in the making, you must look for it.

Remember, it is so important to direct your attention to what excites you, not what scares you.

I find that many women who I coach have beliefs that they are not good enough, sexy enough, slim enough, smart enough. These are just beliefs, and not the truth. The problem is that we start to believe these ingrained untruths- we think 'this is who I am!'

Nothing could be further from the truth, because you are the creator of your life! You can be, do or have whatever you want. Do you believe that? The law of attraction works so well, that if you believe it then you are right, and if you do not believe it you are also right! Because...

Everything that you believe...

is true.

Change your beliefs and your whole world changes!

Today I asked a friend 'Priscilla, what is your dream? She said 'I don't have any idea what my dream is.'

So, I asked the question again. I said to her 'You *do* know what your dream is, what is it that you've always wanted to do?' And in the next breath Priscilla's words literally spilled from her lips ...' I've always wanted to open a vegan restaurant!'

Goddesses don't need to be saved or rescued. They need knowledge of their own power and how to access it.

Chapter 4
The Art of Allowing

The art of allowing has worked so well for me, and it can for you too. It feels far more feminine than the law of attraction. (or at least how the law of attraction is portrayed)

To get any result in life it is important to know that you will need a combination of feminine and masculine energy. Yin and Yang. The idea to bake the cake is the feminine. The doing of it, this is the masculine. Together, the idea and the action create a result.

I first came across the 'Art of Allowing' after I had been teaching about, and studying, the Law of Attraction for many years. People were starting to complain about the book *The Secret,* that it was too materialistically oriented. I did not agree. I felt that people would always ask for what they wanted, and it would be granted, so long as emotionally they could line themselves up to what they desired.

It is so important when manifesting, that you believe you deserve and are worthy, or else you won't receive what it is your heart desires.

Soon after, more publications became available, explaining how important it was that one allows the flow of one's life to happen.... naturally, and without force. 'Going with the flow, moving upstream, everything happening on purpose'.......

I loved these words and I loved this new way of thinking and speaking! I went to a scaravelli yoga class and I remember the teacher saying, as we were in Downward-Dog pose 'allow your heels to be received by the earth.'

Oh my God! Those words opened the biggest gateway for me. I hadn't realised that my fitness and yoga teaching had been such 'masculine language 'of instructions, demands and goals. Suddenly there was no goal, but 'an invitation'. It felt so new and exciting and yet, it was not the language that I'd been taught. The words that I started to use allowed me to feel more liberated and more in touch with my true nature.

Taken out of context, some people mistook this to mean that goals were no longer needed or even required. I myself, stopped manifesting completely for 2 years. I began to listen in each moment what was required, notice my thoughts, my feelings, and act upon that moment. I no longer wanted to live with any structure, lists or instructions.

I didn't know where I was heading. I surrendered my life, started to enjoy my work again (I had no goals, no pressure). I rented out my house of 25 years, told my boys they no longer had a home to come home to when in need (at the time they were 28 and 25 years old), sold many of my belongings, and left the UK for Bali.

I embarked on 2 years of my life with one goal:

No goals, no plans!

When I turned 49, it was time for me to start travelling. I had to turf out the boys who kept using the place as a hotel! Every time they got totally broke because they smoked too much hash, lost a girlfriend or got themselves fired, the bank of mum and hotel 'it's not so bad here' came to the rescue.

I finally decided that now was my time to experience a new kind of life. I hired so many coaches and mentors- all to tell me what I knew deep down. In fact, it took me so much mentoring that the cost started to get me down. Somehow it didn't seem appropriate that a loving mum could deny her children the 'right' to return home whenever they lost a job, girlfriend or got themselves in so much debt (yes, my partner once even paid a huge cannabis debt of for my eldest son so that he would not get beaten up)

Life? Yes, it will test you over and over....

I honour you dear Goddess, right now, right here, for all the experiences you have had. Good, bad and ugly. Messy, heart-breaking, expansive, joyful, destructive, magnificent- they are all part of you and have all made you the woman that you are today.

The masculine aspect always wants to have answers. We, as women have become so caught up in this masculine dominated world that we've forgotten the power in simply listening. Until I started my journey to Shakti wisdom. I hadn't been aware that whenever a friend was in trauma, that I always tried to 'fix' her. I wanted to say the right thing, give the right advice, hold her and comfort her.

One thing that I have learned is that to be fully present with a woman and to allow her to be heard is the greatest gift we can give our sisters.

Take your Playbook and write down a list of at least 5 experiences that you feel that you have really grown from. Next to each one, write a few words that describe what you have learnt from the experience.

e.g. My divorce,

I've learned the kind of man that I want to meet.

My children, I've learned that by encouraging them (finally) to fly the nest that they have grown so much, and it was in fact my feelings of not being needed that in some ways kept them returning home all the time.

Running my own businesses, I have learned how to be financially self-sufficient.

Breaking up from my ex., I have learned that the amount of pain I've experienced after every break up has guided me towards greater self-love. That's been a biggie for me.

Love the process.

Be present.

Once you understand that each moment is exactly as it should be, and you practice acceptance of what is, then you can begin to take *responsibility* for what is. If you start to live by the rule that every problem is an opportunity in disguise, you can immediately begin to shift your focus from helplessness to burning desire. Oh, I do adore that statement! And those two little words! What do *you* have a *burning desire* for? I must just add something here.

Desire very often comes with attachment. 'I desire to be skinny then I will feel more lovable'. Look at the real power that lies beneath the desire. It's called Intention. Intention combined with detachment leads to awareness in the present moment.

When you take action in this present moment awareness, without attachment to the outcome, then you are creating the future through the present moment. If you have a burning desire for something and are not feeling good in the absence of it, then through the Law of Attraction you are pushing away that which you desire.

Can you grab your Playbook and write down 7 things that you have intention (*burning desire*) for?

Before you do this, and indeed every exercise in this book, see if you can take time out to do a short 2-minute meditation.

Shakti Meditation for student Middle-aged Goddesses

Take off your shoes.

Walk outside and feel Mother Earth beneath your feet.

Take in 7 deep breaths

Close your eyes

Move your awareness to your root chakra (around the pelvic area)

Bring your hands, one on top of the other over your heart.

Say out loud or quietly 'Everything I see, I AM'

Open your eyes and repeat the mantra

Notice what you feel.

So, you've done your meditation, you've written down five experiences that you've really grown from. Now close your eyes and allow some (very organic) intentions to bubble up.

Very recently I was clear to myself that I wanted more exercise and more devotional practice in my life. I'd been to 5 rhythms several times locally over the years, and then in the winter of 2017 I had a neighbour, a gorgeous young handsome and very fit guy from Transylvania (think Dracula) and we lived as neighbours in Ubud, Bali. I'd always been a little intimidated by the thought of attending one of the ecstatic dance nights in Ubud. Especially being from a different generation to the majority of dance goers. So, Andreas and I went together.

He was so handsome that everywhere we went, girls would flock. I got to know many women! And it amazed me how many people would come up to me with open arms and tell me that they'd seen me on Facebook! That they 'liked what I said' or loved my tattoos.

I felt some kind of belonging. Weird that at my age this would have such an impact. Or so I thought. I've since learnt that no matter what age or generation, we all need to belong to our tribe. I'd never really felt that connection with people in my local community, a middle-class suburb just 18 miles from North London.

Although I had 'appeared to fit' there is a big live music culture in my home town but it's also the drinking culture that goes with it. Just not my thing.

As soon as I got over myself as being one of the older ones on the dance floor I got lost in the dance. And that's how it was. I'd done enough spiritual practice to not really concern myself with anything other than the pleasure of the ecstasy.

The rhythms, the music, the loving energy all around me and the incredible surge of love pulsating via a strong pounding of life-force energy through my body, connecting me to every other body in that space. This was everything. This IS connection. This is divine love at every level! I was in heaven. I returned to the UK four months later wanting to bring more dance, ritual and ceremony into my life.

After a few months back in the U.K. I was aware that my energies felt unsettled. One night as I lay on my single bed in my little 'outside bedroom' of my house I came across a Facebook advert for an ecstatic dance facilitator course. It caught my eye, so I scrolled down to see that the 7-day course was being offered at half the (what was to become) the usual price. This was appealing, and I scrolled down further to see that the course was to be held at a beautiful ocean side retreat centre in Bali.

Without hesitation I signed up. I'd heard good things about Seth Newman, the facilitator and had even signed up four years earlier for his events via Meetup but never managed to get to an event. In hindsight I realise that the reason I'd never been to an event in London was that I didn't have any friends who fancied going too.

Within a few weeks I was back in Bali and the seven-day course exceeded any expectation I might have had. It wasn't just about the dance, the course incorporated so much more! All the Circling work, authentic communication, workshops I'd attended in Ubud over the winter months, and my years of learning about how to express my emotions - this was the culmination of everything I'd ever studied and experienced and this was the best experiential week of my life! I'd been feeling the immense pleasure that I had experienced through dancing, and the universe, quite effortlessly had bought something amazing to me, effortlessly!

Because I listened to my gut feeling about the ecstatic dance course (I felt excited when I read about the course) I followed my intuition and signed up. So, I followed the breadcrumbs of desire and discovered that one of my intentions now is to become an ecstatic dance facilitator.

So, here's my three. Remember to just feel what feels good as opposed to what you think would be good. Can you notice the difference?

1/ It Is my intention (my burning desire) to finish writing this book and for it to become a number one best seller! It will help other women to realise their full potential.

2/ It is my intention (my burning desire) to move out of my hometown and create a retreat space for retreats and healing at my beautiful home which will be in a warm climate.

(I'm noticing a little fear around this as I write it, and yet my fingers did the typing faster than the fear set in!)

3/ I want more community in my life. When I'm in Bali and Thailand I feel it, and yet when I am home in St Albans, even though I have a Pilates studio at the back of my house and people and teachers coming and going, I feel cut off from my tribe. Since returning from the ecstatic dance Temple Facilitator training in Bali, I finally dared to take myself into London alone to attend a dance event. All those years I'd wanted to go and had never found a friend who wanted to come with me - so I didn't go!

Do you stay at home and not do all the things you'd love to do? Have you lost your confidence? Feel insecure about meeting new people? Afraid to try something and worry that you'll look a fool or won't be good enough? I've noticed lately that I often have to give myself a 'good talking to' when thoughts of 'I can't' creep in.

Coz I bloody well can!!!

Chapter 5
Change Your Thoughts, Change Your Life!

If you want to find your Shakti, then it is important to notice when you have jumped back up into your head.

I love watching my clients, particularly when we're on skype calls taking their eyes up towards their head. What a sure way to know that they are 'thinking' and not 'feeling!'

The body is so remarkably intelligent- and understanding body language is a very useful life tool to have for every Goddess. We need to learn how to listen to the wisdom of the body and not the mind.

Although I talk a lot about learning to get out of your head, it is important to be able to recognise when you are actually in your head- and to notice what exactly is going on in there!

Playbook time

Take 10 sticky notes and write down on every sticky note the following:

What am I thinking?

Now, stick those notes everywhere that you will read them. Bathroom, toilet, car, office, bedroom, kitchen.

This exercise is a deeply profound one, and as well as having done it myself several times, I have had remarkable results with clients too.

Each time you read a note, ask yourself the question 'What am I thinking?' and then answer it.

Start to become aware of what you are thinking.

This is the first step to awakening.

Another exercise to help train you to become aware of your thoughts is to set an alarm on your phone. Schedule it to go off several times a day. When it does, stop a moment and think about what you were just thinking about. Were your thoughts positive or negative? Were you thinking good things or bad things? Check out your body and emotions, too. How are you feeling? Does your feeling reflect what you were thinking? Take your Playbook and write down your thoughts ...

If I'm not paying attention my thoughts can very quickly develop into feelings, and this has the potential to make everything worse. And that's the thing about thoughts. If thoughts come and go, then there's no problem. they don't amount to much. However, it's when we allow thoughts to linger, to develop, to take on more description and more storytelling, that the thoughts turn into actual feelings. That's because:

Thoughts combined with feelings create reality!

That's exactly how creation works. Nothing that has ever been made was made outside of that process.

And really, to be even more simplistic about it: **Feeling creates reality.**

Without feeling, nothing at all is created- ever! Therefore, if we want to become intentional creators of our own reality we must learn to combine our thinking with high vibrational feeling, because this is how we will create high vibrational realities.

What is a high vibrational reality?

We live in a 3D world made up of money, power etc. We are moving at this time in our evolution into a 5D reality (known as a shift or an awakening). In this dimension we are more aligned to love, and the energy of the heart as opposed the 3D reality of the mind (ego). We are all being called to 'awaken' and whether we like it or not, it's where we're heading. It's happening right now! It's why you're reading this book, and it's why your world is starting to change. We are going through an immense awakening on our planet, right now.

The trouble is that most of us aren't looking at our thoughts and feelings. Look at me, I teach this stuff and I still catch myself not doing it! Especially during times of high pressure and stress such as I'm in now, when things are moving too fast for me to realise that I'm thinking all sorts of things, some of which are negative. I'm back from Bali, and as I write I'm aware that 2017 has been the most transformational year of my life!!

Your life so far is a total result of your thinking!!

(Ouch!!!)

Try this exercise:

1/ Make A Habit to Observe Your Thoughts

The mind is always, ALWAYS talking. To change your life for the better you must first change your thoughts for the better, and this requires that you listen to what your mind is saying before the thought came in!!

If you were thinking positively, wonderful. Continue doing so or better yet, steer those positive thoughts with an intention of what you'd like to manifest. However, if you caught yourself thinking negative thoughts, move on to the next step.

2/ Find The part of You that thought the thought.

They are usually expressions of a deeper pattern within us. If we can find the pattern to which they are connected we can also undo it, thus releasing the thoughts and undoing whatever they were beginning to create.

Imagine you just observed yourself thinking, Wow I'm so crap at that! Why do I always get it wrong? I'm such a failure. Without judging yourself or feeling guilty for thinking those negative thoughts, stop a moment and see if you can figure out why you would think those things in the first place. Where does that idea come from? Can you recall someone in your past who said that sort of thing to you, or made you feel that way? Can you recall other times when you felt like a failure, or like you never seemed to get it right? When was that? What was going on at the time?

Take a few moments to trace the history of the thought. Be very observant as you do this, paying close attention to everything that bubbles up, especially intuitive impressions. It's common for a memory to suddenly spring forth, or a mental image to appear in your mind's eye. Pay attention when this happens, because this is literally the picture of the pattern.

3/ Find Yourself in The Pattern

Once an image or a memory has appeared, try to remember where it came from, its origin.

Through visualisation, go into the memory of yourself as you were when this first happened to you (or was said to you); to the space where this belief first began. Find yourself there. What were you wearing? How old were you? Where were you? Who were you with? Hold your awareness there, and breathe...

4/ Rescue Yourself

With the image or memory firmly in your mind, visualise your current self, walking to your past self and then embracing her. Hold your past self; love your past self. Hear as you tell past you that you love her, and that you understand why it is that you've thought these thoughts about yourself, all these years.

Forgive the you that you were then, the one who felt the need to think these thoughts. Forgive her because she didn't deserve to be told a lie or to believe it; forgive her because she knew no better at the time.

Forgive her because you love her — and because you are her.

Allow yourself to be ushered into the light for integration.

Whilst loving your past self, speak to yourself what really is true, so that you can counteract the lie. Your divine higher perspective knows what is true and what is not true. Allow yourself the space to notice what is really true for you, dear goddess.

The truth is: We are divine representations of the God who created us. This same God also lives within us and we are a part of God. Our birth right is joy and peace and prosperity and love and success. That is who we are. That is what is true!

5/ Speak this truth to the past you as you embrace her. Let the light of the truth shine down on the both of you in this visualisation. And as the Light shines, picture yourself integrating the past you with current you. Literally blend the two together until you are one, whole.

You have just rescued, aligned and integrated past you with current you. This means you no longer need to believe the lies — or the negative thoughts emitted from patterns about yourself. You are free.

6/ Steer your thoughts;

Now that you have identified, cleared and loved your way out of negative thinking, it's time to steer your thoughts in the right direction. Imagine your mind to now be a blank canvas where you can begin to choose any thoughts that you wish.

Now add to the mix some affirmations. Affirmations are thoughts with intention, and reflect things you would like to manifest in your life. Once your mind is clear, insert one of these positive affirmations and repeat it several times — if possible, out loud. Doing this allows it sink in.

While sinking in I conjure up a complementary high vibration feeling and amplify it to the best of my ability. Remember how I said earlier that Abraham Hicks recommends that we stay in a high vibration feeling for at least 17 seconds for it to grow and create — so not too long is required to start drawing in that which is the whole of the technique. It's very simple — but also very, very profound. It also has the power to entirely change your inner world, which will then create your outer. You can with practice, do this several times a day for less than five minutes and create lasting change leading to massive transformation!

Let me give you some examples of what your mind might be telling you ....

Like attracts like, so my thinking is constantly attracting people, situations and experiences into my life.

When my energy is expanded, when I am relaxed and 'in the flow' I literally bump into good feeling experiences and situations. Have you noticed how when you go out in a happy mood, the whole world appears to smile at you?

Now let's say you need to go into town to do some mundane job like pay the rent, or buy a hammer. (yes, those are very dull sounding to me!) So, you look in the mirror and you say to yourself

'God, you look fat today! And those wrinkles are getting deeper.... I never have any time for me anymore...... I feel tired........ why didn't Suzie call I wonder.... I mustn't forget to give Henry his tools back.... I am stressed!

Now see if you can observe all those thoughts. How do they make you *feel*?

Can you give yourself some space between what your head is telling you and notice how you converse with yourself?

Do you recognize that you are programmed to self-criticise, constantly judge, and put crazy undue pressure on your beautiful self?

Do you remember where it came from?

So many of us have been *programmed* to believe from a very young age that we are not quite *good enough*.

What did you parents tell you?

I was lucky in that I had a grandma who taught creative dance 'music to movement' and encouraged me to move and express myself.

Until the day she died, in her late 90's her favourite saying was 'do me a dance!'

What are your memories?

I usually only remember the not so good feelings around my refugee, Hungarian father and his lack of empathy. Today, right now, I celebrate the good feelings I received from Grandma.

My love is no different for either as both have taught me and both have shown me love.

How I choose to interpret and receive it is up to me.

So, take your Playbook and write down 10 *positive* statements for yourself. For example:

"I am a beautiful woman, I am ready now for change, I am loving myself more and more each day, every day I feel stronger."

If this feels like too big a step then try 'I am becoming a beautiful woman....'

It is always possible to take a baby step in the direction of a better thought. There is nothing wrong with negative thoughts but in time they will accumulate and turn to feelings. Feelings come about through repetitive thoughts, so if we can become aware of our thoughts then we can take responsibility for choosing them. However, feelings are real and felt in the body- and to simply 'think positively' when you are feeling down, depressed or upset would be deny their very existence. A feeling becomes an emotion. Energy in motion- and the best gift of healing you can give yourself is to allow yourself to feel the emotion. Covering it up with a 'happy thought' will not allow the energy to move through you. The energy gets literally stuck in the physical body and in time turns to a depletion of energy, symptoms of malaise and disease.

Now, get yourself a big sheet of drawing paper, some coloured pencils or pens and make a big poster of one of your affirmations, draw some flowers or anything else that makes you feel good, and stick the finished picture on your wall or fridge so that you can see it every day.

Becoming a Goddess requires that *all* of you is allowed. Like every single bit.

The negative as well as the positive. See how you feel about your perceived problems or mind chat once you can separate yourself from believing that they are you.

You are not your thoughts! You are Not your thoughts.

You are Not your thoughts!

Great Goddess, show me how to release the limits I impose on myself.

Now get off your ass and go buy that hammer....

Chapter 6
Finding Your Shakti

Shakti is your creative life force energy and she is desperately wanting you to connect with her! When you do, you'll feel liberated...... ecstatic, present, alive, orgasmic, joyful and free!

Dear Goddess in the making, I invite you into a sacred world of rediscovering who you really are.... And I promise you, you won't be disappointed!

If you have ever had that longing to touch, taste, feel life on another level... that irritating and sometimes depressing feeling that you are somehow looking through a window of life and not fully living your own true reality, not even trusting that there is more than you are experiencing, then I invite you into my blossoming, ever-unfolding world of getting to know your true self.

An inner world that majestically mirrors on the outside that which you create on the inside....... It's like a world within each world, an unfolding rose where the scent becomes sweeter as I unravel each petal.

Shakti, Goddess energy is pure creativity! Embrace! Ideas can come to you through daydreams, inspiring talks, books, people, dreams...

Anywhere, anytime!

'When the world is ready to accept and act on an idea, everything materialises, people, so called 'coincidences' meetings, connections, everything begins to unfold, moves in conjunction ... as if totally on purpose, everything flows in the 'right direction to bring that idea into actuality.'

The thing that may be preventing you (because I know siStar how very naturally creative you are) is your anxiety to fully express your creativity. Anxiety is a feature of the human condition. It is a much larger feature than most people realise. A great deal of what we do in life, we do in order to reduce our experience of anxiety or in order to avoid anxiety altogether.

Our very human defensiveness is one of the primary ways that we try to avoid experiencing anxiety. If something is about to make us anxious we deny that it is happening, make ourselves sick so that we can concentrate on our sickness, get angry at our mate to have something else to focus on, and so on.

It is the way that we make manifest our potential, make use of our intelligence, and embrace what we love. When we create, we feel whole, useful, and devoted.

Unfortunately, we often also feel anxious as we create or contemplate creating. We get anxious because we fear we may fail, because we fear we may disappoint ourselves, because the work can be extremely hard, because we may be rejected, and so on. We want to create, because we know at our core that it is the most awesome thing to do and to feel, and yet we also don't want to create, so we don't have to feel this anxiety and the embarrassment of failing or 'making a fool' of ourselves! That is the simple, profound dilemma that millions of women find themselves in.

The thing to do is to become an anxiety expert and get on with your creating! As we say in Heart IQ, simply notice the thoughts in your head, the feelings in your body, the judgements, the criticisms- and do it anyway!

I had a client recently who came to see me in an attempt to stop drinking so much wine. With an exhausting full-time job as an accountant, and two young school children, the glass of wine had become 3 or more glasses a night. I asked her what was it that she was 'stuffing down' to stop herself from feeling. She responded that she was often anxious. Underneath her anxiousness was a longing to fit in. She felt that by drinking she could literally curb her natural Goddess Shakti energy and 'fit in with the rest of society.

This beautiful 42-year-old woman was so desperate to fit in, that she was willing to consume alcohol to stuff down her feelings about who she really was. Living in a large detached home with 'nice respectable neighbours' and all the trappings of suburbia, at a very core level was not living as her soul longed for. She was not truly being who she really was.

Many women (and men too) get to this point. I don't believe in a 'midlife crisis' but I do believe that at some point we get to the thought 'there must be more than this!'

"I think midlife is when the universe gently places her hands upon your shoulders, pulls you close, and whispers in your ear: I'm not screwing around. It's time. All this pretending and performing - these coping mechanisms that you've developed to protect yourself from feeling inadequate and getting hurt has to go."

Your armour is preventing you from growing into your gifts. I understand that you needed these protections when you were small. I understand that you believed your armour could help you secure all the things you needed to feel worthy of love and belonging, but you're still searching and you're more lost than ever.

Time is growing short. There are unexplored adventures ahead of you. You can't live the rest of your life worried about what other people think.

You were born worthy of love and belonging.

Courage and daring are coursing through you.

"You were made to live and love with your whole heart. It's time to show up and be seen."

~ Brené Brown

So, Shakti baby, what will your next creative project be? Or can you return to your current creative project with a new willingness to accept the reality of anxiety? To help reduce your experience of anxiety, remember to breathe deeply, speak positively to yourself, and affirm that your creative life matters to you.

If some anxiety remains, create anyway! Your Shakti, your life force creative energy, once tapped into will become your greatest magical power. You will feed your soul; your longings will be fulfilled. There is no other way to bliss than to tap into *her* energy.

So, my beautiful, what would you like to create? A painting? A meal, crochet, novel, an idea?

Once you can notice what literally gets your juices flowing, then you're moving towards your next creative experience. Name it, talk about it, feel it, research it, join a group about it. Once you are clear what it is that you want to create, the universe will start helping move you along towards your creation.

I want to help prepare you for this, and it is important to start noticing the smaller manifestations in your everyday life. Perhaps you've already noticed more so called 'coincidences'. These will become more and more apparent the more you get into the flow and connect with who you really are.

In your Playbook, write down 3 ideas (or more) of things that you would like to create in the next 3 months.

How does it feel to write it down? Can you literally allow yourself to visualise this wondrous creation of yours?

Spend 30 minutes daydreaming about what you would like to create.

This will include some aspects of an earlier exercise and you may find it all starts to merge into one. That's OK! I call it play rather than work, because when you earn a living doing what you love to do it no longer feels like work.

And.....

True Shakti energy can be a little chaotic too!

An old friend returned to my town a few months ago after living in the south of France for ten years. She'd moved there with her young son after her mother died and wanted to begin a new life. She'd always loved France and spoke the language well. She bought a small apartment with some inheritance money and worked as an estate agent.

Once her son began university she decided it was time to move back home to the UK. But she was fed up with work and wanted a career change. She told me 'Liz, I believed for a moment that I was too old (56) to find a new job, so I thought long and hard about what I would do for a living. I wanted to find work where I could earn good money and work for myself.' So, she decided to train as a tattoo removal and hair remover laser therapist.

The course was under £2000 and when she turned up for the weekend's training each participant was invited to share their professional experience. She felt herself sinking into her chair as each student proudly claimed to be 'a plastic surgeon', 'a medical doctor', and such like. She felt embarrassed that she was a single parent and had just quit her job as an estate agent and was looking for a career change.

She told the group that she'd just returned to the UK after 10 years living in St Tropez - and they were so impressed by her story that no one asked her about her work!

But she had done her homework, discovering that tattoos are on the increase and that a high percentage of people regret having them and so removals are also on the increase too. This career change was a stepping stone for my friend to assist her in her new life and giving her confidence as a soon to be business owner.

Now think about the following:

What do you look like? What are you wearing? Who are you with? Where are you? What are you doing?

How is the weather? Is it a natural environment or a city? What's the look on your face? How are you feeling? Please make a list of all the emotions that you are feeling.

Also, notice any negative feelings, any sentences that might come up for you. As you write your perfect experience, write these negative thoughts down on the next page.

Example: I am sitting in a nice restaurant with my ideal partner, sipping champagne and designing a new clothing range with a girlfriend, (yes, please dream BIG). Notice any negative thoughts arise such as ' I am too fat to design nice clothes,' or 'no one would ever buy my clothes because I am not good enough'.

Goddess Julie

I want to tell you about an amazing Pilates teacher who took my very first Pilates teacher training course in 1999.

Julie contacted me to say that she'd seen my teacher training course advertised online, that she would love to train in Pilates, but that sadly she was overweight, and not at all sure that she had the body confidence to teach Pilates,

She was already teaching fitness, and due to a medical condition that she had, was unable to lose weight, even though she ran miles every day and stuck to a good diet.

She described herself as 'big'.

Talking to her on the phone, I felt the compassion in her heart, the yearning to teach, the amazing personality, the great sense of humour and the willingness to overcome her doubts (or she would not have contacted me in the first place!)

What Julie was looking for was approval. She didn't feel good enough.

I want to tell you that since Julie did my training she has become a *very* successful Pilates teacher, running retreats in Europe and with a strong following. (Nor was she as 'big' as she had described)

Julie has excelled, and is now looking to open a new Pilates equipped studio. Not only that, after being dumped twice by boyfriends after 7 years (always 7 years) and having been told that she could not have children, she met and married her soulmate, and adopted two beautiful children.

This has nothing to do with (and yet everything to do with) what I am writing about right now .... but I MUST share with you how she met her man.

Julie was feeling *rubbish*. Her last boyfriend had told her he didn't want to marry her, after 7 years of hoping that he would propose to her... exactly the same scenario as her *last* relationship.

She was feeling low, and decided to go and see a great friend of mine Peter King, an awesome life coach and NLP practitioner. She told Peter what was going on for her, and that session told him that in the evening she had been invited to a large birthday party in a restaurant. But the only thing was that there were sixteen other people invited to the meal, all couples!

Whatever Peter gave to Julie that day (a powerful meditation) she came out feeling as if she was the most beautiful woman on the planet! When she arrived at the pub before the meal she was trying to get her new mobile phone to work. A guy at the bar made a joke and they spoke a few words. Later, when they got to the restaurant all eight couples sat opposite each other and Julie was sat at the end of the long table with no one opposite her.

One of the guys stood up and walked to the table of men next to them and said, 'Who would like to come and sit opposite my friend here?' (I would have died with embarrassment, in fact, I wouldn't have even shown up!)

To Julie's surprise, up stood the guy who she'd chatted to in the pub earlier. They didn't stop talking all night, started dating, made a beautiful connection, married a couple of years later and Julie and he adopted a beautiful girl and boy, the children she was told she would never have.

That story could be your story.

Don't let 'your story' of too fat, too thin, not clever enough, not lovable enough, too frightened, too incapable, too, too, too...... YOU fill out the words that sabotage your dreams, your goals, your excitements.

And now we must let go of those beliefs.

It's time.

Transformation is yours for the taking beautiful Goddess. I will hold your hand and we can walk together into the light of truth.

Chapter 7
Getting Real

There is a massive misconception in the self-help, personal development industry that all lightworkers of the world (including the magnificent *you*) are meant to be happy all the time!

The perception is that people that are 'walking their walk' are doing so without ever messing up.

Not feeling happy all the time, eating cake, and not floating around on some golden lined fluffy cloud in the sky most of the day! This isn't how it is at all and it's not how it's meant to be either...

Listen here, Goddess.......

I have had my biggest and most *profound* leaps in growing spiritually always following some of the lowest points. In fact, *hand on heart,* I can tell you that my very lowest points have brought about the deepest transformations.

I've got to an age now where I no longer need to read about these truths, because I can now state them as my *own* experience.

What times can you think of in your own life when you had very low points and then had major breakthroughs?

It's like over-eating. One day you have just had enough, and you say to yourself That's it! I'm done with this. It really is time to look at my emotional needs. Making changes in your life is not about a new way of being *forever*. Small baby steps are taken in the direction of your chosen path. That is how lasting change happens.

And dear Goddess.......

IN Joy the journey!

Don't ever let *any* feelings of negativity, going backwards, feeling low, angry or any other feelings that come up for you, make you think that you are lost in any way! These feelings are all part of being human. Of being a *Goddess.*

In fact, as every teacher that I have ever had has said, we need to embrace all our feelings- including the negative ones. I love how Christian Pankhurst, creator of Heart IQ, describes our shadow. He talks about inviting a friend over to our house. Guests arrive, and we greet them into the beautiful living room. 'Welcome to my lovely home', you say with great pride.

But there are a couple of rooms where you keep all the stuff you don't want, don't like and they are dark and messy. You have absolutely zero intention of inviting your guests into these rooms! But, to heal, to integrate the shadow part of you with the light, we need to show all our rooms, and allow the feelings of shame, guilt and embarrassment to be felt.

This is how we heal.

This is how we awaken to our divinity!

The true teachers out there have a deep understanding that shit hits the fan in order for them to grow 'spiritually'.

It's a profound, sacred part of being human that enables all teachers, all therapists, all women, to experience the fullness of life in order to teach new perspectives to their students, fellow workers, families and friends.

So, *Goddess,* I want you to pay particular attention over the coming weeks to times when you feel as if you're going 'backwards'.

Since beginning my journey with Heart IQ I have grown *so* much. Feeling very down happens much less frequently now since I started really *allowing* all my emotions to be fully expressed and loved. Starting my own *Heart Circling* groups enabled me not only to facilitate groups, but also to experience being in circle. It is *very,* very powerful.

I found that *Self-Love* has had a massive impact on how I feel from day to day.

As I have peeled away layers and practiced self-awareness this past two years more and more I am now choosing to put the *true love* for myself before anyone. The only reason ever that we feel like we're going backwards is because we have come out of alignment from our highest truth. (I didn't used to understand what this meant, so I'm going to explain it very clearly.)

If every human being followed this simple rule, then world suffering would cease immediately!

Be in alignment with your highest truth.

This does not mean that your truth is what your parents wanted for you. Nor your employer, your best friend or your spiritual Guru. You see the thing is, most of us have been unhappy because we haven't been real. Yes, it's simple! But how do I know if I'm real or not, you may ask. OK, let me help you out a little. Because ultimately, this is what this book is all about! It is so damned simple

Being real is SO damned Sexy!!

When you are real, and remember who you are, then you connect to your Goddess energy!

Here's the thing. Society has entered your being so deeply, what your parents taught you, spoke to you about, has penetrated you to your core. So, it's no wonder that you became confused! Even if they are now deceased, your parents' words still live on in your head.

Whatever they told you still speaks to you in subtle whisperings inside your head. The parental voice has become your ego. If you do something to upset this, it will condemn you instantly. And if you do what it has taught you well, oh boy, will it appreciate you! Your mother, father, teachers, religions, have all built up this 'conscience' and it has now become your bondage.

Conscience is given to you by others who want to manipulate you. They have not manipulated you on purpose, because they were tortured like this by their own parents, by their own societies and religions. So long as you have these voices in your head, you will never experience the richness, the awesomeness or the memory of who you *really* are.

Twenty years ago, when I was desperately trying to heal myself of my life's big trauma I sought many therapists and spiritual teachers. I wanted to find the '*chosen*' one who could help me heal.

I searched through directories, magazines and asked everyone and anyone I could think of. It's quite funny now to think that in those days we couldn't simply '*google it*'. But, had *googling* it been an option then this would not have worked either. In fact, it probably in some ways could potentially make it more challenging because there are so many people 'out there' claiming to have all the answers!

What I am sharing with you is my own personal journey to awakening. What I know is that with the right ingredients it *is* possible to heal and to wake up to the truth of who you are. And remember dear Goddess, whatever you believe...is true.

So, I remember getting a lead about a 'spiritual guru' and celebrating with myself. '*At last, I have found a guru!* 'I met the woman twice and could not afford the train fare to London nor the extortionate cost of this woman's offerings to heal me, to heal my soul and to guide me to the light. But then back in those days, I put so much emphasis on the *cost* that I was already bound by *negativity.* And my desperation to find a guru was acting like a repellent.

Ha, I see that now. Isn't hindsight a wonderful thing?

Some of the 'gurus' that I contacted claimed that their therapy 'was the best' whilst others told me to '*go inside*'. That what I was seeking was inside of myself. *Damn it*! I had no idea what so ever how to do this.

For years I made attempts to 'go inside'. But I just couldn't get the hang of it. My body, mind and soul were riddled with post-traumatic stress disorder, I was often bedridden for months at a time and I felt that I finally had the family that I'd always longed for, a new husband whom I adored more than life itself, two amazing boys – and now my health was suffering!

Damn- I wanted it all!

Learning TM (Transcendental Meditation) was a step forward and helped me to relax my traumatised body/mind, and this I am convinced relieved me, even if only temporarily. I always felt good after TM, and it was this practice that enabled me to control my anxiety attacks.

I'd often sit in my car when I felt panicky in the supermarket car park and meditate for twenty minutes. Actually, looking back, my meditation practice was a life saver! It worked so well, and I practiced twice daily for many months. I guess I should have kept up my practice once my strength came back, but I didn't.

Instead, every time I had a bout of adrenal burnout (which usually lasted around 3 months) I would come back to my meditation, my deep rest and my super healthy eating. This became a pattern for over 15 years.

I was dealing with the trauma surrounding the death of my first husband, and yet now in love and married to a truly beautiful soul who was sadly another addict.

They say that it is only possible to love another to the degree in which you love yourself. So, I was smoking around thirty cigarettes a day, and loving my new husband and my beautiful little boys the hardest I possibly could. If I look back now, I see a lost soul who was desperate for love. That is why she had children, that is why she married twice. She did the best she could, given the set of circumstances that she was handed.

And I love her.

It is only when we begin to live from our authentic self that life really starts to flow.

And part of my flow was illness.

I really had to surrender.

I see so clearly now that my relationships could never have given me the real deepest love that I craved, because I could not find it for myself. If I cannot find that love, that real deep love for myself, then I can never give it to another.

So many are '*putting up*' with relationships that are not serving their highest truth. Are you?

In my marriages I put up with so much. Addictions were the norm. I knew deep down that it wasn't healthy bringing up my children with an alcoholic, but I loved him, and certainly wasn't prepared to put my boys through another loss. And addicts are just everyday beautiful living people, like you and me. They've just lost connection to the true self.

I know someone who says she loves herself very much, and she even goes so far as to say that she wishes she could have a best friend who is just like her! Yet, she is in a relationship with a man who is not compatible with her. She is even stalling her spiritual and personal development because 'the timing is not right.'

But, I believe that there is no such thing as *waiting* to become authentic.

When your heart speaks to you, it speaks *truth*.

It is the mind that keeps us stuck, we don't feel good, we fall victim to our circumstances, we don't feel in control and so to feel in control we create lives that are controlled.

Every single week I meet women who are not feeling authentic in their relationships. They don't have the strength to address the most important questions to life itself. They work to set routines, cleaning, OCD, shopping, games, gym, running.... or they drop into depression.

Anything not to *feel*.

What it is that you do to numb yourself from how you feel?

Take your Playbook and write down your top 3 numbing activities.

Since writing this chapter it's now summer 2016 and it's been a weird one. In fact, it's made me realise that I need to hurry up and share this book because life changes so much with all this wisdom that I need to get the work out there to you!

Facebook has been a helpful medium for me to share. I am trusting enough in the process to know that me being vulnerable gives others permission to drop into their own vulnerability. And so, it is.

I want to share a Facebook status with you that I wrote recently on a small raw food/fruitarian help group I belong to.

September 2016

My eating habits this past month have been worse than ever! It seems as if every time I go raw or fruitarian the worse I swing the other way when I 'collapse'.

Last weekend my son got married on a TV show. It's top secret at the moment so I can't say anymore! My younger son was flown in from Oz to the UK.

Their dad died when they were babies, 30 years ago and their step dad was an alcoholic! I was triggered several times into very deep unconscious triggers/wounds and noticed that my response was to eat sugar/ wheat. I was shocked at my inability to use any of the tools that I have to keep me from experiencing such strong emotions.

The wedding was brilliant, but exhausting and we have a wonderful new family of in laws. But my emotional pain, body and my eating habits have left me feeling out of sorts. My comfort has been cake, scones and coffee. I came home to an empty house (the same house the boys grew up in) and initially it felt unbearable, after spending time with my sons and my family (we all stayed up north where my eldest lives with his new wife, who is part of a lovely big vibrant Geordie family!)

I am slowly coming back into synch, and leave for my winter travels in 6 weeks or so and feeling calmer today. Thinking about fruit again but knowing that really, I ought to come off comfort food and coffee for a while before beginning to attempt going raw again. Last time a few months back I had the worst detox symptoms I have ever experienced, vomiting, diarrhoea and splitting headache! As usual I seem to be all or nothing!

Oh, by the way I was also really disappointed that the timing of my son's wedding meant that I missed the second part of my (£1000 worth) heart IQ practitioner course! So, I missed my week in Holland, which I'd been looking forward to all year!

I love food so much, it's also my comfort when needed, and yet I feel so alive, vibrant and connected when I'm fully raw.

I just wonder if my emotional body will allow me to maintain raw. Thanks for listening and allowing me to share. Please keep the TV thing secret as it has to be kept quiet until it's aired in the spring. And please, I'm not really asking to be 'fixed' rather just heard and acknowledged, Thank you.

Take your Playbook

Imagine that you are now free to write your most honest Facebook status ever! Imagine that you do not care who judges you because you know that the one who judges, is only seeing himself/herself and feeling his/her own insecurities. What would you write, right now, today?

Feeling safe enough to be vulnerable, to share how we really feel, is so enormously liberating!

Many years ago, I attended a fitness conference. I always attended the mind - body workshops and talks, which were totally new areas of study in the fitness industry in the mid to late 'nineties'. These conferences would attract fitness professionals from all around the UK and beyond but the 'mind body' lectures were always very quiet compared to the hundreds that would gather for sessions such as step or 'funk fusion'.

On this particular occasion, I was coming towards the end of a bout of chronic fatigue and I was deliberately choosing the easiest gentlest options. But I was also fascinated by anything to do with spiritual growth and development. The lecturer (whose name I sadly don't remember) read out a piece at the end of the workshop that had the biggest and most profound impact than anything I had ever heard before in my entire life! Yes, this piece, written by Marianne Williamson literally changed my life!

Our deepest fear is not that we are inadequate. Our deepest fear is that we are powerful beyond measure. It is our light, not our darkness that most frightens us. We ask ourselves, who am I to be brilliant, gorgeous, talented, and fabulous? Actually, who are you not to be? You are a child of God. You're playing small does not serve the world. There is nothing enlightened about shrinking so that other people will not feel insecure around you. We are all meant to shine, as children do. We were born to make manifest the glory of God that is within us. It is not just in some of us; it is in everyone and as we let our own light shine, we unconsciously give others permission to do the same. As we are liberated from our own fear, our presence automatically liberates others.

Something changed profoundly in me after I heard those beautiful words at that incredible workshop over seventeen years ago. And It is my deepest wish that as you read this book, and even after you've read it, that you keep it by your bedside, and that you pick up and randomly open up at any page, and that the words in this book will help to be a catalyst for your own transformation too.

Even the thought of that sends shivers down my spine. When we are touched at our core by profound truths that the heart recognises - something incredible happens. We become liberated!

Freedom is love, and until I can fully be real with myself it is impossible to fully love myself. So, the more real I am, the more love I can allow to flow through me, inwards and outwards. The greater my vibration emanates out into the world, and back again, the more magical occurrences show up into my experience. Become the greatest version of you!

Because the more real you become, the more you give others permission to do the same.

Empowered women

Empower Women

SiStar..

I am another you,

In L'akesh.

Chapter 8
Your Ideal Life

Have you ever imagined your ideal life? It does fascinate me that so many of us middle-aged Goddesses do imagine our ideal life, but it feels so far away that we abandon any real thoughts with more dominant beliefs of unworthiness. In fact, the single most reason that I hear from women is this. 'I don't believe I am good enough!'

When the 'real you' wants something then she is drawn to people, places and situations that will support her. Your intention is already there, or you would not be reading this book. But- what does your ideal life look like? You will need to discover it, and it will be a process of discovery.

I ask you to notice your dreams,

and to feel into the quality of your longings.

As you begin to reconnect with the deeper aspect of who you really are you will begin to blossom and reignite the flame within. Reminding you of your essence, your inner being, your truth, you will look younger and you will radiate a beauty that cannot be bought from the purchase of a new pair of shoes!

If you jumped in your car right now, without knowing where you were going, you may end up going in circles. But if you had a destination, then that is different. It may take you a long way to get there, perhaps many detours, but you would have a place to reach.

I worked a lot around NLP, goal setting and structure when I used to have a life coach back in the early noughties. But at that time, I was unaware of how strong the masculine aspect of routine was not only driving me, but also causing me to feel as if I was failing should I not manage to stick to my committed practice of waking early and having a very structured timetable.

In my forties I had a great life coach who would get me to write down my goals and to set myself a structured week. So, I was to be up at 6.30am (I hate waking up that early) I would go for my power walk (adrenals and running are no good for me) whilst listening to empowering speakers on my headphones. Even in the winter months I would do this, not daily, but the routine felt good. It was some years later that I heard about the Law of least effort.

Have you heard of one of the Universal laws called Law of least effort? I was so excited when I discovered this universal truth. I use it on a daily basis. Especially when I'm feeling stressed or overwhelmed. It's like my guru. I'd like you to get a really good 'feel' for this law. So, let us say that you have a dream to open a little teashop. You are pushing and pushing, financially, with your time and your effort. You are tired, exhausted even because things are not going to plan.

Let Go

Let God

Sometimes, you just have to let go and trust. Your practice today is to go to a beautiful natural environment, daydream, smell the roses. If you can't make it today, don't worry. Take your diary and make a date with yourself to go and simply hang out in nature.

Spend time with yourself and allow thoughts, ideas and feelings to flow. When we really let go then magic starts to happen. New energies gently tap us on the shoulder, hey girl.... you remember me? You remember how you used to get excited about.... being in love, starting a business, exercising.... you fill in the blanks.

Don't be in a hurry. Don't push. All the lessons that you need will come forth and you can embrace each lesson with love. Don't assume that obstacles are there to piss you off as at first it might seem. I really know about obstacles. But again, how would I know the stars were shining without the dark night sky? When we connect with our deepness, we can trust that all is exactly as it is meant to be. When we worry, judge and label……. Hell, yeah that will feel sooooo restricting!

GO

With

The

Flow

siStar

What are you longing for? Have you ever given yourself permission to ask what your heart truly longs for? The feminine heart is by nature a longing heart. In the very depth of our longing we will never be truly satisfied unless we find a way to honour and share our creative self. The feeling is often an expression of a deeper longing: the longing to shine as who we truly are. When a woman finds a way to give from her heart, her frustration disappears. She feels fulfilled because she is connected to and shares from the very source of that which she thinks she lacks. The longing to "give of ourselves completely" to go "deeper", is infinite and when truly honoured and met it can become the greatest gift. So, I dare you dear siStar……

Give what you most long for. If you long for more honesty, BE honest. If you long for more power, BE powerful, if you long for more Love BE more loving.

Whatever you think the world is withholding from you,

you are withholding from the world.

What I longed for more than anything else in the entire world was a partner to travel through this life with. Having never been in what I would call a 'conscious relationship' (see chapter 22), I knew deep down that in order to have the relationship that I longed for then I needed to first find that very relationship with my own self. Actually, dear beloved siStar ....

That's a lie.

I was told time and time again, through books, courses, exes (who could've taken some of their own advice) that I needed to 'find myself '.

What was so scary about this concept (a word I rarely use, but to me then, it was a 'concept') was that it would mean that I would be required to spend significant time on my own, not being in a relationship nor searching for a partner. That was the biggest challenge.

Let me also point out that it is possible to 'find oneself' whilst in a romantic partnership but the partner would need to be pretty conscious to allow the space required for personal and spiritual growth.

So, I began my journey to Self. I started to attend transformational 3-day courses, and started to really believe that I could make my dreams come true. My ideal life seemed like a long way from where I stood in my shoes, but it intuitively felt like a journey worth taking. And compared to the life that I was living, which was kind of borderline shit and mediocre with some splashes of rampant passionate, surges of massive enthusiasm, I decided to give this 'finding yourself' malarkey a go.

"The day came when the risk to remain tight in a bud was more painful than the risk it took to blossom."

-- Anais Nin

OK, so what have you written in your Playbook?

Can you start to think about your ideal life more often? Fake it until you make it? Yes, I absolutely believe that faking it until you make it works! I get my clients to do it all the time, it's real, it works, do it!

I remember after completing my aerobics teacher training I was feeling excited to be looking for a job in a local gym. I was nervous and feeling some resistance to not 'looking the part' for the prestigious role at this brand new exclusive health club.

I approached the gleaming doors of the beautiful brand-new state of the art health club and literally walked through the door, smashing my face against the large glass panels and nearly passing out as I staggered up to reception! I felt dizzy and sick and I was directed up the stairs to the dance studio where I taught 2 back to back classes for two hours. I waited afterwards for my assessment, having given my all and with a bruised face too! It wasn't too long before I realised that nobody had actually been in there assessing me -of all the cheek. What they had really wanted was a cover teacher for cheap, I felt used and unworthy and I never heard from anyone about the possibility of work at that fitness centre again.

So what I decided to do some years later when I'd had myself a little experience in teaching at another gym, was to literally 'act ' like I owned the place as I walked through the doors of my new audition! I told the friendly studio manager that I was a yoga teacher even though I had never done a yoga class in my life! I had simply bought the new Jerry Hall video that was being promoted on the TV in the early nineties. I learnt a few postures and headed off for a meeting with the nice sounding studio manager after making sure that I wouldn't repeat my actions from before. (I've been scared of glass doors ever since) I walked into the building head held up high, I had given myself a really good talking to, and decided that I would 'act with an inner knowing that I was a good and experienced yoga teacher'. Not only did I get the job as first Yoga teacher in a St Albans gym, but the studio manager and myself became best friends!

Fake it till you make it, siStar!

Chapter 9
Goddess of Sensuality

Having stupendously random, sexy and awesomely strikingly, beautiful ideas are one of the greatest experiences known to a Shakti Goddess!

Let me ask you something...

When did you last dance naked?

A Goddess will find pleasure in this because dancing naked is authentic, alive and real!

I honour you dear Goddess, right now, right here, for all the experiences you have had. Good, bad and ugly. Messy, heart-breaking, expansive, joyful, destructive, magnificent, they are all part of you and have all made you the woman that you are today.

The sad fact is that of all the thousands of women who I've worked with, coached and connected with, very few of them have been able to connect deeply with their own sensuality. Even some of the world's top coaches, helping others to manifest, create and achieve in other areas such as business or marketing have this area of their life untapped.

When they reveal this 'minor' piece of information, as if it's barely worth mentioning, it sends chills through my spine. Our very essence is sensual, and it is the very portal to our awakening.

Once we can access our sensuality then we connect with the juiciness of life. Once we have experienced this level of richness, life becomes something quite different. I talk more about this in my online course 'How to meet the Love of your Life'

In recent months I have made the huge decision to shift my work from teaching Pilates and yoga to empowering women to connect to their sensual shakti energy, through embodied movement, breath and heart circles. It feels to me that this is what is most needed on our planet. And in this way, we are also giving our sons and our brothers and lovers a chance to connect to their divine masculine.

Sensuality is a key ingredient to living a life of joy and bliss.

'The Goddess of Sensuality is adventurous and not particularly quiet. She was the girl at school who couldn't stand still in the dinner queue and wore the wrong uniform. She needs to move constantly, and dislikes being stuck in one place. She thinks with her body.

She's the one who moves her pelvis whilst watching her child perform in the school performance and sings along to the chorus forgetting that she's the parent and not meant to be participating! She's a free spirit and her work is creative and a reflection of who she is. You won't find this Goddess in an office, and if she is in an office, she knows full well that it's time for her to release herself from the prison of her restricted life and start becoming her true self.

Her skin is radiant from the healthy fresh foods she chooses to eat. She likes to bare her shoulders because she's more comfortable feeling the sun on her body and does not wear less clothing to look provocative but because it feels most natural to her, as a girl she was often told off for going barefoot, and as a woman she still enjoys feeling the sensation of the earth beneath her feet.

That girl was me.

Can you claim her? And if not, what stopped you? What were your conditionings and beliefs around sensuality?

Some of our biggest blocks are around our passion and sexuality. Sensuality has been forgotten. Tantra and other natural practices are slowly re-emerging. Personally, I'm not convinced that all the men holding space for Tantra, especially those with any kind of 'guru' status, are conscious enough and enlightened enough for practices such as a yoni massage. But here's the thing; you do not need a man to connect deeply to this energy. This life force energy is ours, and we can experience it with divine pleasure without needing to be in relationship with anyone other than God.

Having said that, I've spoken to women who've had incredibly healing experiences from receiving a yoni massage, where other therapies have not hit the spot (pardon the pun). Particularly helpful it appears in cases of sexual abuse where the yoni has closed down energetically.

The most powerful energy that we have is Shakti energy.

It is vital that every woman connects with this energy in order to remember who she really is. It is vital that the blocks that have been created are set free so that you, yes you, can enjoy your sacred sensual self!

Playbook Time...

Take your Playbook my beautiful Goddess and write down 5 reasons why you would not want to dance naked (alone) and five reasons why it might, just might feel really liberating.

Close your eyes and really imagine it. And later today or tomorrow or this week I invite you to do it. And you know what? I shall do it tonight too. Allow your 'inner teenager ' to be embarrassed, notice your 'inner critic' and ignore her , feel into your 'inner sensual Goddess' and tease her into sacred playfulness!

When you can come back to some basics of being alive, and remember who you really are, getting real will happen effortlessly and you know what dear sister it may not be a smooth ride. But enjoy the journey because that's all you have. And it will be worth it. I promise you.

I'll definitely be having new editions to this book, because I'm learning so much, so fast.

As I write these particular words (some chapters have been written with fifteen-month gaps, ha ha) I have been exploring ecstatic dance and contact dance.

What I am learning is that as we let down our barriers and remove the mask, we open ourselves up to deeper levels of joy, love and connection. Not just to self but to everyone that we come into contact with.

As you begin to explore who you really are, you may be drawn to attend some Tantra introductory workshops and sessions. Please be aware that I have coached women who have been deeply traumatised by the experience. I have attended sessions, and in all I do have concern that in some cases, a gap needs bridging between the experienced tantric master/facilitator and the 'average middle-aged woman.'

I do actually feel quite strongly about this. Having said that, I do believe that the tantric path is a beautiful spiritual journey definitely not to be missed!

Shakti Malan (who has sadly passed since I wrote these words) in particular is a beautiful soul who I would definitely recommend listening to on YouTube.

The most important rule in Tantra is that you are very clear with your boundaries. There is no right or wrong, it's all about asking yourself where your edge is and checking in with yourself. I haven't yet met a man who is so conscious that I would trust him. And when I did trust a man, I regretted the experience the next morning.

I certainly am not here to put you off. But I want you to feel supported siStar in knowing that you can become the Goddess without the need to attend any special groups, activities or cults! You will become so much more aware and intuitive that you will begin to 'feel into' which path to take on a daily basis. And you may well choose Tantra, because at its purity, it is not about sex, it's about life itself.

I met a guy in his sixties on Facebook and we shared many friends. I could see and feel that he was a man of integrity and love. His posts were just divine and he appeared to live by his deepest truth! A wise man to be respected. I had several healing sessions with him over the years by skype as he lived in a small town in Southern Europe. I knew that he had helped so many women not just from Europe but also in Australia and the US. I was delighted when he said he would be visiting London for a seminar and we agreed to hang out for a few days. I had a spare room and I was excited to talk to him about his tantric practice and learn more about this ancient sacred philosophy on living an embodied and fully integrated abundant and juicy life!

I met him at the airport and was surprised to find that behind the Facebook mask, and even our skype sessions, was a very quiet, shy man. Humble yes, and I was immediately wondering how I would entertain a guy for two days who was so almost awkwardly inward. I offered to do the touristy 'thing' of accompanying him around the beautiful Roman city in which I live, with its abundance of fine dining & cultural treasures. But he insisted that he just wanted to spend time in my presence, and treat me like the Goddess, which he knew I so needed and craved! On the first evening, after dinner, he sat next to me on my sofa and then as our hearty conversation dropped into a deeper presence, Guy (not his real name) sat at the floor by my feet. A big part of me wanted to move away and yet I knew the 'work' of this amazing man and I wasn't going to let my fear and shame around feeling inhibited and shy stop me from experiencing the work of a tantric master. A man whose grace and presence had inspired me for over three years, someone with whom I shared many conscious friends around the world.

As he stroked my feet and then my thigh I felt an overwhelming urge to move and protect my body from his gentle and yet powerful advances. He spoke with such wisdom, and tenderness that it was challenging for my head to get around this unusual situation.

I felt unsure and yet excited. I told myself 'you've taken on this Goddess role, added Shakti 'as a middle name and you can't even find the power to consciously conduct yourself with this beautiful light being.

I chose to ignore the dictating going on in my head and to allow myself to let go into the unfolding mystery. As the evening continued, and our conversations on philosophy and life deepened, I found myself getting exquisitely turned on by the stroking and had I not had the self-control I think I might've regretted what would have or could have happened next.

I gently pulled away and we said our goodnights. I wondered how the rest of the weekend would pan out- and it didn't take too long for me to find out.

The next morning Guy agreed to my insistence of a quick visit to my beautiful little city but he seemed agitated to not be spending time simply 'be-ing'. I was doing my very first fruit fast and my body was feeling trim and toned. People think that I am always this way but the truth is that I've had a major sugar addiction my whole life and the only photos that you'll generally see of my body are when I am 'being good'. I have had the same body issues as so many other women, and the shame of my bum, thighs, legs, breasts, skin has dramatically improved in the past ten years or so, thank God! But the thought of a man seeing my flabbiness (unless of course we are totally and completely in love) still to degrees fills me with dread. No makeup is cool with me, but my body......... ummmm no way Jose!

I felt incredibly amazed that Guy had said that for the duration of his short stay, he would join me in eating fruit only. I was a little surprised but took the gesture as being another offering of gratitude and appreciation of our connection. Guy was a man who'd been in a marriage for over fifteen years and this made me feel safe to spend time with him. I was always so very wary of men and their ulterior motives. It's like when you've had a male friend for some time and then you discover that they've been very attracted to you. I think I had a little autism in this department! I noticed that I was already wondering what the evening would bring, and I was curious about the gift that Guy spoke of. I knew that he had many clients for his shamanic/tantric work and that he agreed with me in many ways about modern tantra being overtly focussed on sexual practices and not enough on the original sacred scriptures, which were not nearly so sex-focussed.

If I'm totally and completely honest (which I try to be as is humanly possible) I did have an inkling of what the gift might entail. A part of me felt annoyed that it had been taken for granted that I would even want to receive this 'gift'. It reminded me of an ex-boyfriend whom I overheard tell an old acquaintance that him and I would be getting married! Really? You didn't even inform me yet!

So the evening approached and I felt a sense of excitement in my body. Like my higher self knew that something quite deliciously unspoken was on the agenda, and that my mission now was not to jump into my head and rise up into fear.

I'd attended some tantric workshops over the past few years, and I was very aware of my comfort zones. But my Goddess energy was ready for new barriers to be broken. And I had the perfect gentleman to assist me. The thing was, I had noted whilst attending women's' groups, and other gentle practices, that this type of tantric work was attracting many whom had either been abused, never orgasmed or were just pure damned horny and willing to try anything! Well I didn't fit into any of those categories, and so I needed to check in with myself exactly what I was going to be 'up for' during my offering of loving heartfelt presence from an overly generous man who proclaimed to work in service to the Goddess.

As the evening drew near I felt clear that I was going to receive something pretty amazing. After all, Guy kept telling me 'I want to gift you with something special' and the intrigue, as well as the excitement of the potential that had awakened in me the evening before, assured me that this was possibly going to be a night to remember. So long as I could just simply keep out of my head and go with the flow.

And trust.

Practice cultivating your intuition and living by your own truth!

Perhaps my mind had been working overtime on trying to guess what this precious gift would be. I discovered that it was a massage, and this felt very safe. A delicious massage from a tantra teacher with heaps of experience and paying clients! And I felt in great shape too, for a fifty-four year old woman. My years of simple exercise had paid off and with the eating plan on a roll I had to admit even to myself, that I looked pretty hot for a middle-aged mother of two adult men!

If anything I felt wasted. Wasted that I could be looking this hot and no one to adore me, to appreciate the whole of me. Not just my looks, my body- but my very essence. Oh, how I was longing for intimacy in a fully committed relationship! And there are many conscious beautiful, intelligent women the world over, trust me, looking for the same: to meet their Shiva.

So I don't actually remember how the evening began but what I do remember is acting all cool and agreeing to lie on my big double bed and insisting on keeping on my knickers!

Feeling trim really did make a huge impact on my confidence, and suffice to say, had I been lying there in my usual body I would no way have agreed to this 'experiment'.

Guy assured me several times that this was not a sexual experience for him and that his mission was simply to serve. That he had been put on this earth to serve the feminine, and that the women he works with have incredible emotional breakthroughs. He told me that he intuitively always follows his guidance and callings. I completely trusted Guy and felt held as if we were in the most intimate of relationships.

What followed was a very sensual massage that I really gave myself permission to fully let go into my senses .There was a voice in my head asking 'isn't this kind of intimacy reserved for my romantic relationships' and another voice saying 'shut the fuck up and enjoy!'

It was wonderful and I was quite proud of myself that I'd allowed this man into my sacred place, a man full of love and compassion for the sacred woman.

I slept really well and the next morning I awoke and asked myself what I had allowed. The part of me that felt my higher self-appeared slightly unsure. I questioned over and over. Was it my inner prude showing up? I so wanted to be carefree around this subject of tantra, I wanted to 'know' what I believe to be the most beautiful sacred expression of the divine masculine & the divine feminine. And here I was the morning after feeling some regret and shame.

Our final day together and when Guy stroked and gently caressed me this time I actually had feelings of violation and of him invading my personal space. I thought to myself 'if, lovely gentle man, you really are so consciously aware, wouldn't you in fact pick up on my uncomfortableness?'

I was relieved when I dropped him at the train station. I knew that he was a genuine man, I am an empath and I feel people. There wasn't a bad bone in his body. He was real. However, a few weeks later, after ignoring his emails of thanks, or at least keeping them short and to the point, I decided to do something that I teach others to do. Something that I practice in order to stay in my integrity and my truth. I decided to be honest with Guy and tell him how it really was for me.

Below is a copy of that letter and I have removed 'Guy's' real name for privacy.

Dear

Sorry I've not been in touch sooner. I've been pretty busy and I needed time to process my experience/time with you. I wanted to message you and say it was great and I really enjoyed our time together. And that is absolutely true in part. But I cannot say that it's 100% true and I would feel a fraud if I didn't share with you the truth of how it was for me. So I am going to see if I can express how it felt for me in a way that feels very real and authentic and I hope that I don't come across in anyway as attacking, because that is NOT my intention.

When you asked to come and visit me I felt honoured that you wanted to come and hang out. I thought of a few places we could go, friends we could meet and so on. It became apparent when I met you that you are, as you said, an introvert. And that you wanted to spend your time with me alone (or that's how it came across anyway). I was unaware that you were a tantra teacher' but was fascinated by this and happy to talk on the subject. However, you said 3 times that you would love to offer me a full body massage and also told me about your all night immersions- to which I felt I needed to be clear that I was not interested in experiencing this kind of thing.

I am very comfortable with my sexuality, my ability to orgasm easily, and I'm not aware of any psychological issues either on this subject. I was very aware of the intimate nature of your caresses on Thursday evening and on Friday evening when you again mentioned your desire to offer me a full body massage I decided to experience it, along with whatever else. Yes, I was I guess interested to know what all the fuss was about re. a yoni massage.

The next morning, having very much enjoyed the pleasurable aspect of the night before, I wondered why I had agreed. For me, it has confirmed that I choose to keep my pleasure sexual activities to someone whom I am both physically as well as mentally attracted to. I felt almost that you had come with an agenda (rightly or wrongly this is how I felt) and that I had agreed to experience something on offer that I really now regret if I'm honest!

It was as much pleasure as I can give myself, and the experience didn't leave me feeling richer, happier or more of a Goddess. In Fact the opposite. I felt almost violated. Even with the feeling of safety and honouring of my female body- I felt violated!

I couldn't even admit this to myself. It felt really powerful for me when I had the realization that I couldn't respond to your message - because I wouldn't have been speaking my truth.

I felt that your 'introvertedness' uses a defence by connecting with women at this level. And obviously many women like this and get a huge amount from it. But it didn't do that for me and I am sorry that I am writing this. But relieved that I can speak my truth.

I know that this was NOT your intention. However it feels important for me to share this with you.

On the Saturday evening I was extremely uncomfortable with your caresses on my body and was surprised that you didn't pick up on this. I am a very tactile person, however I was uncomfortable with your assumption that it was ok to stroke my thighs without me having any say. It felt really uncomfortable. Again, I am happy for this with another when there is a mutual attraction. That's just me and I felt that my personal boundaries were crossed. Beliefs or not, it felt like it was all about what your needs were as a sensitive tantra heart felt teacher!

Whatever or however you feel about me saying this, I need to express.

I love you as a human being. This is why I am choosing to be honest with you.

Liz xx

I felt such a powerful relief after sending this email, which was spoken from my absolute truth.

Here is the response. I am very confident that no one knows who this guy is and my reason for sharing is a powerful one. I want other women to always feel into what feels true for them! My soul purpose is to serve.

Funny, I actually meant to write 'my whole purpose is to serve' but the word 'soul' was written.

Dear Liz.

Thank you so very much for speaking your full truth to me! Yes. It was difficult for me to read this. It has stirred up a lot in me.

First and foremost, I am so very sorry to hear that this was the experience you had. I am so disappointed to have inflicted my unconscious "shadow" upon you. It concerns me that I was not nearly as attuned to your discomfort as I need to be! Quite frankly, looking back, I was clueless. Until this email arrived, I remained so. And that is not normal, nor in any way acceptable for me!

As I feel back into my entire experience – from the moment of meeting you at the airport – it feels to me as if I was in some kind of light enchantment of my own making. Probably a product of several factors involving jet lag, anticipation, my own sense of being honored by your hosting me, and a deepening appreciation (the more I heard, saw, and sensed of you) for your brave, beautiful, and radiant Self.

My self-conscious self really hates to admit it, but if I am rigorously honest with myself, there probably was an agenda that began to unconsciously formulate itself over time. I'm sure it was all with "noble intent" – the desire to serve and celebrate you. But clearly my sense of what would be truly "serving" and truly "celebratory" for you was distorted by my inexplicable failure to really listen to – and honor – yours.

I absolutely needed to hear this from you!! This work demands continuous checking and re-checking of my state of consciousness and intentionality. I had probably been starting to slip into a form of complacency. I was clearly due a solid "wakeup" call. And you were probably the "perfect" person for me to get it from. With your clarity, gentleness, and unapologetic honesty; and a voice I would really hear.

So even though it hurts my human heart to know this was the experience I actually created for you, my wiser soul knows the importance of my hearing your truth, experiencing the relatively gentle wounding to my sense of self, and remembering to never relax into believing "I know what I am doing." And so I really mean it when I say thank you. I really mean it when I say I am sorry.

I am hoping that, ultimately, this will not do any lasting damage to the quality of our connection. I assure you I will never slip into that sort of unconsciousness with you, again! I have no interest in perpetrating any form of imposition upon you whether consciously or unconsciously. Nor upon anyone, which is why your "intervention" is particularly valuable to me.

I love you, honor you, and am quite vulnerable to your discernments ... So thank you for your kindness in stating this so clearly for me. I will treasure this lesson.

Namasté

PS: Upon further reflection, it seems that at least some part of me was aware of your discomfort, as I intentionally did not move into a full "yoni massage" experience. Even then, it took your clear "I feel complete" to ensure I did not "go there." Ah the lessons to be gleaned. I will try very hard to stay in the sadness I currently feel in my heart ... and not "spiritually short-circuit" my human process of grieving, learning, integrating ... Thank you, again.

I feel that offering your sincere feedback was (is!) an act of love. Thank you, Liz.

Love you!

Pretty powerful, huh? As I copied and pasted these emails and then re-read for the first time since receiving them in May 2016, tears rolled down my cheeks. Not for what happened, but for the open hearted depth of honesty in our communication. For me, this is tantra.

So perhaps it's nothing to do with trusting a man or not. Perhaps it to do with trusting our own intuition, our own truth and expressing it lovingly.

And as I re read this chapter several years on, I now question 'was my shadow somehow playing out ' 'was I unclear in my message of wanting and not wanting?' And the biggest lesson simply being this; that we are all just human beings doing our best. Being conscious doesn't mean getting it 'right '. When we are in touch with our sensuality and when we can share it with another, it is a beautiful experience. But are we as women clear about our boundaries and in sharing our truth?

Three powerful lessons:

1. Everyone is our teacher.

2. Take responsibility sister, and always share your deepest feelings.

3. Be true to yourself and the whole world benefits.

This is ultimate sensual intimacy.

Chapter 10
My Health Journey

I remember standing in the hall of the house we lived in. A dreadful piercing pain shot through my belly and I fell to the floor in agony. A sore throat that had developed months earlier was not going to stop me going for my audition to The Royal Ballet! But as my symptoms worsened, and I became exhausted beyond anything I'd ever known, my GP suggested that I take time out from school.

I went to stay with my grandparents in a country village in Lincolnshire and was spoilt rotten.

From the moment that my ballet teacher had told me that she wanted me to take an audition for the Royal Academy she had made it clear to me that I was too tall.

My parents' heights had to be entered onto the application form and unless I was to be cursed by some odd freak of nature, then it looked certain that I would follow in their footsteps.

When I saw my audition photograph I nearly died at the sight of my backside. It looked way too big for the slim elegant 11-year body that I was wearing.

When my mother went in to tell my form teacher, we were both shocked when the tall, skinny, Religious Education teacher asked if Elizabeth 'had asked God for help?' How crazy was that in 1972? Both my mother and I thought that the RE teacher was insane.

For 3 months I rested with my grandparents and gradually was allowed to attend half days at school. I went for test after test and was eventually diagnosed with a little-known disease called Glandular fever.

Fast forward fifteen years. After my first husband died a friend took me to an aerobics class. They were becoming all the rage in the mid-eighties, and I found that the relaxation at the end of the session gave me a sense of peace that was rarely experienced.

I was generally living on alcohol and cigarettes. My new husband loved to drink too, and sadly this seemed to be the focus of our lives.

When my aerobics teacher told me one day that I had a real gift for dance and suggested that I train as a teacher I was completely shocked. I was the would-be ballet dancer with the huge behind. How could I ever go into the fitness industry? The industry for skinny girls with pert bottoms.

When I attended my first day of training, a room with large mirrors and ballet bars greeted me. We did dance routines and I felt so exhilarated. In fact, I felt as if I was on the set of Fame.

I'd waited for this for so long! I didn't even own a pair of trainers, removing my Doc Martens before each class I'd attended to dance barefoot. I was treated like the odd one, and I felt different to the others. It wasn't about the trainers for me. It was about having the freedom to express myself.

After an intense 6 months I was ready to take my exams and become a fully qualified aerobics teacher. At 28 I hadn't really trained in anything apart from fashion, and how to deal with major grief and become a mum to two vibrant little boys.

As we prepared for the exams I was teaching my much-practiced routine to the other would-be teachers in the large YMCA dance studio. I'd recently remarried and it felt like after 2 years of intensity that my life was slowly getting back on track.

As I stood in front of the class ready to teach I noticed that I felt very weak. I couldn't find the energy I needed to move. I guessed I was coming down with something.

Weeks went by and I didn't get better. I had to take my exam sitting down and instructing my class (I was told that this skill was the makings of a great teacher.) Months went by and my energy wouldn't return.

After about 6 months I seemed to recover. I'd been to every doctor in the practice, tried every medicine, and nothing worked.

When I organised a sponsored workout the following year I put myself under so much pressure. I organised a raffle, collecting prizes, choreographing new routines, promoting. I was completely exhausted!

Living on cigarettes and adrenalin really took its toll. I was also over exercising and teaching around 15 classes a week. The day after the very successful sponsored workout, I collapsed in a heap.

I couldn't walk, I went to bed for 2 months and fought like crazy to get better. It was like having the worst flue ever, that never went away.

In between my on-going bouts of extreme exhaustion, I continued to work as an aerobics teacher and personal trainer. Sometimes I would spend weeks at home sitting on the sofa and other times I would need to put my personal training clients on a step in their lounge rather than run the streets with them. Where there is a will there is a way.

Every 9 months or so I would get an attack which would usually last around 3 months. This particular time was the worst so far.

Someone had advertised a new exercise machine in a new beauty salon. It was a free offer and you could go and have a toning session to try it out and see your muscles work without putting in the effort.

My sister and I decided to try it out. Because my muscles were so toned I couldn't feel the vibration of the machine on my muscles.

The therapist had to turn the machine to full power in order for me to feel a mild sensation!

From that day on I felt as if I was plugged into an electric socket. My nerves were on edge and I called it the *jangles*. I had my first panic attack and started suffering with anxiety. I couldn't go into large shops or open spaces. At my very lowest point I lay completely exhausted in bed and I was so scared because I'd never felt so weak in my life. I didn't know how or where I would find the energy to take in my next breath.

Exhaustion of the adrenals is not something that anyone can even begin to imagine. You have to have actually experienced chronic fatigue to have the slightest clue as to how severe (and real) this is.

I was eventually recommended an Indian acupuncturist. I'd tried a reflexologist and that had given me the flue the very next day! (I later discovered that was actually a positive sign of shift happening)

So, when I sat with this lovely man and went through my history and told him how I'd been to the hospital for test after test he looked at me with very kind eyes and said something that felt so real. Something that I'd waited to be told for such a long time, that not one single doctor had told me about.

'Elizabeth, you have endured massive amounts of stress. Your adrenal glands have burnt themselves out. You have all the symptoms of Post-Traumatic Stress Disorder!'

I'd seen so many doctors and specialists over the course of the past few years and not one of them identified my illness and exhaustion as anything to do with my adrenal glands. I lay on the bed with needles sticking out all over my body, the curtains were drawn, relaxing music played. And by the end of the session a miracle had occurred.

For the first time in a round 6 months the 'jangles' had left my body. I felt at one.

This experience changed my life forever.

Over the next twelve years adrenal burnout would find me, usually after heightened periods of stress, and sometimes months after the event.

Sometimes it appeared out of what felt like nowhere. But slowly I learnt this: Instead of fighting to get better and wishing away a few months of my life, I decided to surrender to it.

I managed to get through a divorce and although unbelievably painful for many years, my soul knew that the parting was another step on my journey to living a more wholesome and heart-centred way of living.

Eventually I recognised the onset of burnout was coming whenever I over exercised.

Fluey type symptoms always preceded full burnout, and I learnt how to recognise the signs very early on and make the necessary life changes immediately.

I met Teejay in 2001 and our 3rd date was a 3-day Anthony Robbins seminar. Teejay was into personal development on a big scale, as well as nutrition and supplements.

I'd done some life changing courses already and now I had a partner to share my passion with.

A few years later I was diagnosed with inflammation of the bowel which developed into ulcerative colitis. My mother was given two months to live and the stress bought on the most debilitating version of colitis. I lost so much weight and I thought I was going to die.

My mother had been diagnosed with bowel cancer after bleeding had not been checked by the GP, and now I had the same. I was put on medication for life and told that I had a high chance of dying young too,

My father had also suffered with colitis and was living with a colostomy bag. And my grandfather had also died from cancer.

We opened our new Pilates studio at the back of my house, and to be honest, it meant very little to me in the greater scheme of things.

I was planning my funeral, not the forthcoming success of an expensive and impressive building at the back of my house.

In 2010 I decided to stop taking medication for good. The GP had warned me that without it I had a 70% chance of getting colon cancer.

But I seemed to clear it myself through a huge (but gradual) change in my diet and lifestyle. I was now getting a flareup of colitis about once every 10 months or so.

And what I believe caused it in the past few years was when I was attending healing workshops I would literally be triggered into a memory of the trauma of my late twenties.

I would imagine I was actually in the scene, feeling all the repressed feelings that at the time I wasn't able to deal with.

Although I had cried for what felt like years, I think that the hash and the alcohol had just served as a temporary measure of self-numbing.

The pain was still buried deep in my tissues and when invited out was uncontrollable. This would then lead to a flareup of colitis.

What is your health journey? Take your Playbook and write down all your health issues and any associated feelings, thoughts, plans to heal and what steps you can take to start (or continue) your health journey.

The more I chose to live my life as the real me, the healthier I became.

Ultimately, we are all one. We are all connected because God resides within us all.

We have an ego (mind) and this ego believes that it is separate, that it has an identity, and that one day its time will be up.

The ego knows suffering very well. And it is very, very scared of dying. The soul knows differently.

The soul has been around for many, many lifetimes and is not afraid of death for it knows that all that dies is the physical body. The soul is expressed through creativity, such as dance, art, music. How would you choose to express your soul?

Have you tried ecstatic dance?

This year I have gone to the next level of healing. I knew that in order to heal my gut I needed to revisit my grief .so I signed up for a 'deep dive' intensive weekend with Christian Pankhurst, the creator of Heart IQ, whom I trained with throughout 2016. That 3-day event marked the beginning of the deepest form of release that I've ever experienced!

During my online training and on a previous live seven-day retreat I'd witnessed the dramatic release of deeply stored emotional pain and trauma. Although I knew that I'd experienced tremendous grief after losing my first husband I'd never actually felt anger towards him. It was in there somewhere, but it had been so insanely overpowered by grief - grief for the loss of my children's father that any feelings of anger had been completely wiped out. Even in the previous retreat with Christian I'd felt the pain of other brave souls as they yelled and screamed but I just wasn't quite able to access my own longing to release.

In heart IQ we use some methods similar to gestalt therapy. I'd seen (mostly women) use the process for expressing anger towards fathers who'd sexually abused them or mothers who'd starved their young daughter of love. It was an incredibly moving experience to watch. If you've heard of a therapy called 'Family constellations', it's a little similar, though perhaps not quite as brutal!

Every time any of the guys was expressing rage, or even simply raising their voices I was getting triggered. On one powerful exercise I felt my body actually turn to stone. And the exercise that was taking place was not even about angry men as such. It was simply any man expressing anger that would trigger me deeply. I literally 'switched off!'

Once the exercise was over, and I was starting to come back into my body I started to become aware of how many memories I had of my ex-husband shouting, usually when drunk. Never physical violence, never over long periods, nothing like some women experience.

However, 'small' and 'insignificant' it seemed by my rational mind, the impact had buried itself into my subconscious. Imbedded itself into my cells. But there was another anger still to be expressed. This anger didn't quite know what or how, but it was there. Fortunately, I'd done the training, I'd seen others lead the way, and I knew what was possible during a Heart IQ experience! Christian invited me to 'take the stage' so to speak. I knew that my time had come to release one of the heaviest burdens of my life.

Gut wrenching, soul destroying, pain and trauma. I held you for so long, because I knew how others suffered so much more. Rape, incest, murder, disease.

But the language of the Heart showed me how I could meet my rage without putting blame on the other. Moreover, it allowed me to access my fire. Once I accessed this heavy burden that I'd carried for thirty years, it felt like the heat was rising up from the pit of my stomach and was released via my throat with my voice. So, this is what happened;

I had to choose a man from our group (there were around eight guys and maybe twenty women) I chose the biggest, strongest man. He was wrapped up in pillows with heavy duty tape. This took about twenty minutes. There must have been eight or so pillows covering his torso. I was handed a baton, I was about to access the anger that I'd never actually expressed. The anger that was lost because Steve, my first husband was sick and then finally diagnosed with cancer before I'd ever had a chance to even think about getting angry with what had happened prior to his illness.

So here I was, standing in the middle of a huge room surrounded by about thirty people and in front of a big guy covered in protective armour and holding a baton. It was surreal, and I felt nervous. Having studied *Heart IQ* I already knew that I was to 'fake it until I made it'. Something I teach myself, but was surprised to know that it was also relevant in awakening buried emotions.

Within literally a minute I was able to access my deepest and most long held emotions!! Taps from the baton turned to whacks turned to yells, screams and finally total rage! I was shouting and screaming all the unexpressed pure sheer rage, anger, torment and frustration I'd experienced whilst pregnant with my second son. All aimed at Steve, who had been throwing his weekly wages into the pub fruit machines every night, instead of coming home to his young family. I beat him with my baton as I screamed 'you FUCKING bastard' over and over before eventually running out of energy as I sobbed ... 'I was pregnant, and I needed your support!'

I had never in my entire life imagined that I had so much anger to release! I knew it was buried so deeply and that, so much sadness had been present, but having the opportunity to let it all out in one swift bashing - well, that was a process worth having. I was exhausted, but I knew that I had released a huge burden from my energy body. Probably the biggest release of my life that I will ever have.

Chapter 11
The Goddess of Healing

Like with any spiritual practice, real change comes not from adding to the many courses and workshops you attend. Nor reading every spiritual and personal growth book. Although these provide insights and offer support, ideas and information, real and lasting healing comes from doing our 'inner work'. My invitation is for you to use this book as your manual and dip in and out of it whilst taking some time out for your inner work. Your inner work may initially be simply making a promise to yourself to spend 5 minutes in nature every day.

I had a partner for five years when my boys were in their teens, and four years after my divorce to my second husband. My partner and I would joke that he owned every single course, book and boxed set of every single personal development teacher out there! I do remember him lying down and listening to the hundreds of pounds worth of hemi sync meditation music for a few weeks. But apart from that, I think he thought that because he'd purchased the goods then the work was done!

I have been similar in many ways, although to be fair, I think that, as I keep on saying, we can only move forwards in bite-sized pieces. Otherwise all can be lost. Real change, real depth, real inner work takes time. Having said that, sometimes deep profound shifts can happen in a heartbeat, and we find that we can never truly be the same person again.

Healing must include mind, body and spirit. In fact, the cells of the body only recognise pain as pain. They don't say to themselves 'Okay, this pain is emotional and this pain here is physical.' All pain comes from an emotion. Emotion comes from the words 'energy in motion.' When an emotion gets trapped in the body over time it will cause pain. It's the same with stress. The cells of the body only see stress as stress. They're not really interested in where it comes from.

My biggest breakthrough came on Jan 23rd, 2015. I finally stopped smoking, after a forty-year battle with my addiction to nicotine. This for me, marked the end of a lifetime of self-hatred. It sounds pretty severe, doesn't it? But the times I could've given myself a tenner for each time I disgusted myself beyond belief, I could've bought a brand- new Land Rover!

It was that bad.

I have had first-hand experience at realising the enormity of the power of addiction.

The 'mother' wound

One of the most important healings we can give ourselves as women is healing the mother wound. The mother wound is the pain of being a woman passed down through generations of women in patriarchal cultures. We literally take on the DNA of our ancestors. We also take on the dysfunctional coping mechanisms that are used to process the pain. What was your life like with your mother? Do you still carry unresolved pain?

Dear mother of mine

You gave me life

So, I could feel,

So, I could breath,

So, I could be

You showed me how

You showed me why

And you showed me

What I didn't want

in my life!

Thank you, dear mother.

I Bow to you

Shakti Kali Kaloczi

When we can heal our mother wounds, we free up our daughters and our sons too.

In our patriarchal, culture women are conditioned to think of themselves as not worthy and this feeling has been passed down through generations of women.

When a daughter takes on her mother's unconscious beliefs she is in some way betraying her own future potential. Through loyalty and as a survival mechanism the daughter will internalise these limiting beliefs unconsciously simply to win her mother's love and approval.

What was your relationship like with your mother?

How aware are you of the dynamic that played out between you?

How has your life been impacted by your own mother wounding?

My own mother shocked me as on her death bed she confessed her sorrow at being such a controlling mother. I was speechless, distraught and intrigued. For many years after her passing I thought about her final words, the love in her eyes and the depth of her final words "I love you so much" didn't equate to a controlling mother. The deeper I looked the more the unconscious memories became conscious, but as with all mothers my mum did the best she could with what she had. What she did have was a very controlling Hungarian husband. Throughout my whole childhood I never understood with how she put up with him and I never wanted to be like her.

If you'd like to know more on this subject I highly recommend the work of Bethany Webster. I consider Bethany's work to be quite unique in this field.

And the father wounding ....

My own personal wounding, like so many, has been most significant around my father. Yesterday I went to visit my father. It's my 'duty' to go and see him twice a week, on Tuesdays and Fridays.

He's 82, Hungarian, blind and very depressed. He won't go out and visit people even though he has a vibrant personality and doesn't look his age. When I was a young girl my father would tell me 'Elizabet, (think Hungarian accent) you can take away my arms, my legs but never, ever do I want to go blind! If God ever takes away my sight I would rather die!

So, for the last seven years my poor father has lived in hell. Yesterday my dad did something he's done regularly throughout my life. He upset me, cutting, brutal, unforgiving can be our parents!

After a lovely two hours of me listening to him talk about his favourite subjects of politics and football, a long walk and a cuppa, he proclaimed 'you are on the bottom of the heap Elizabet!'

I was so taken aback that I stood up to defend myself. But my breath was wasted. This man believes that all my friends are on drugs, that the reason I used to go to Thailand was for prostitution, and that I am the most unsuccessful of my three other siblings.

As much as I adore my father at the deepest level, his words cut me like a knife. How could my own father think this of me?

Now I hear my unconscious self, feel so sad for herself, that she never got the love from her father that she craved. But how many of us do? How many of us really get the love that we long for? siStar, are you loving yourself?

Ironically, last week I reached out to my own mentor and teacher and we had decided that it was time to look at healing my father wound. How perfect! It was as if the universe had recognised that the work was about to be done and so had given me a massive 'here you go!'

Here's something to get your teeth into!'

So, we're looking at the conditions in which I was conceived, energetically what I came into being with, and how I was imprinted rather blueprinted with various energies. Thank God that nowadays women generally don't get labelled with such demoralising words!

The whole experience yesterday (and my subsequent sharing on Facebook) has reminded me of how much I really did have to endure as a young woman who was desperate for the love of her father.

Take your Playbook

What is your wounding? What do you recall in your life in relation to your father? Where do you feel your memories? Which part of your body? Can you speak to the pain? What does she tell you? Can you allow the tears to flow?

Isis is the Goddess of Healing. As the protector of women, Isis helped women in childbirth and comforted women when their loved ones died. She shows us that women have great reservoirs of strength and inspiration.

Isis reconnects us with our innate healing powers, and so is beloved by healers. She supports everyone's quest to reclaim their individual power and take responsibility for their healing journey. She shows us our ability to heal ourselves and to heal others. Isis can help to awaken your healing abilities and healing intuition, your ability to communicate with the physical body and to intuit any needs you may have for healing.

When was the last time you connected with your own innate healing powers? Have you spoken with her? Listened to her? Isis empowers you to use the healing power of love and gratitude and to raise the energy level of the physical body by connecting to source.

From the moment that you were born you started to have experiences that at the moment of the experience, you were not fully able to embrace, nor fully able to feel. For example, as a small child your father may have told you off because he was in a bad mood over an argument with someone at work. In a very short time we get confused with our emotions of 'not feeling good' because we were told off. But we get confused and we start to believe that our feelings are who we are. In other words, instead of just simply realising that our emotions are simply 'energy in emotion' we believe that we are bad, not good enough and not worthy.

This is where core unworthiness comes from. We literally get programmed to not feel, to control, to contract, and to withhold. So, if we didn't feel fully accepted and fully for who we are what often happens is that in relationship later on, this fear of being rejected comes up, and sadly (think 'law of attraction') What we most fear often comes to us.

Grief can take on many forms. As women with a fear of being rejected we often attract men who will do just that which we fear. So, when a relationship breaks down we will literally grieve the loss - sometimes for decades or even a lifetime.

Unlike in ancient times nowadays we are expected often to hide our grief, to get back to work the day after a funeral. We have forgotten how to mourn, how to honour the process of grieving.

Isis reminds us that grief is a powerful part of our experience in life and should not be repressed. Grief that is not expressed can eventually become physical disease and or mental illness.

I have recently been working with Sarah. Sarah became pregnant at 14 and had to nurse her mother who was dying from injuries sustained from Sarah's father. When Sarah's mother died Sarah and her new baby became homeless. She was offered accommodation by a family where she was abused. Sarah was unable to grieve for her mother. Instead she drank to stuff down her feelings. Feeling was too painful, and she had a baby to deal with. Fast forward thirty years and Sarah is finally mourning the passing of her beloved mother. The tears are finally flowing. She knows that without the release of the blocked emotions that she will never truly heal. Alcohol is a great way to block healing!

So, you can see that it's really important that we clear our past. We can never move forward and create the life we desire whilst still carrying our traumas from the past.

We cannot change what has happened, it's part of our story. But we can work on releasing the negativity around it.

Last year I worked with a woman who was diagnosed with a personality disorder, depression and anxiety.

I never plan a session because anything can happen. I was thinking that we would do a one on one heart circle session but after a relaxation we both became very aware of spirit in the room. I'll call this client Milly.

Milly had been sent to live with her grandmother at an early age because her mother was an addict. Milly had never felt that her mother really cared for her. She had gone on to have a child of her own, but the father walked out whilst she was pregnant. She felt she had psychic abilities and started meditating but found that her environment didn't really suit her.

During our session Milly was able to tap into some unresolved wounds and she began to shake. We both felt the presence of her great aunt who gave her some messages. Tears flowed, and feelings that had been trapped for over thirty years were finally given a safe space in which to be felt. At the end of the two-hour session Milly felt an aliveness that she hadn't experienced before. Her headache had lifted, she felt lighter and she was moved to tell me that she was ready to forgive her mother.

Take your Playbook and write down this invocation to clear the past.

I call upon the Infinite Mind; The Prime Creator; The Source of All That Is.

Repeat this, 3 times in silence and Creator will be in your presence. Then you declare to Creator, your intent to do so. You would say:

It is my intent to clear and release ____________________ (name the emotion, feelings or thought patterns that you want to clear and release), then you would declare the following invocation:

I claim it.

I own it.

I created it.

I lived it.

I loved it.

I learned from it.

And no one can take it from me, not even Creator.

Then you release it by your own free will, since you recognised that it no longer serves you for your highest good. You release it with the Intent to send it to the Light of Creator. You now declare this by saying:

"I now release it by my own free will, for it no longer serves me for my highest good and I send it to the Light of Creator, to be changed back to the Light."

A word on forgiveness...

In order to clear your past and heal your heart it is essential to forgive all of those whom you believe have 'hurt' you. Being able to find compassion and forgiveness is a reflection of spiritual maturity.

Holding resentment is only hurting yourself. It is directed inwardly and will ultimately cause dis-ease in the body. The very first 'spiritual' book I ever read was Louise Hay's 'You can heal your life'. In it Louise describes all the associated emotions with each bodily ailment. If you are new to the subject of forgiveness I highly recommend that you read Louise's book.

Another great book on the subject that I keep as my bible is Debbie Shapiro's 'The body mind workbook'.

You must start truly cultivating a practice and a desire for liberation! Forgiving is essential if we are to heal. It's not about pretending that difficult things didn't happen. Forgiveness doesn't mean transcending the wound. Forgiveness asks us to really allow grace in to lead the way.

To join another in a place that is deeper than the personality, to join from the depth of our being to the depth of another's being, when we begin to awaken the Goddess, we notice the ease of these practices beginning to 'fit'. Everything takes practice and needs cultivating with love and tenderness. Be aware of when you start to judge yourself too. Keep going back to the chapter on 'what am I thinking?'

SiStars .....remember......

Practice makes perfect.

Childhood Wounding

In order to live from our true self, it requires that we revisit some of our deepest childhood wounding.

Take your Playbook

What parts of your authentic self, did you have to hide or try and cover up in your childhood? See if you can remember where you felt small and insignificant. What parts of yourself are you not expressing? Can you take yourself back to childhood, your earliest memories and revisit similar feelings? Try not to push any uncomfortable thoughts and memories away.

Once you've written some memories down put down your pen and allow yourself to drop into your feeling body. Just try to fully observe any sensations in your body, as if you are simply the witness of them. Take your time with this process, and allow any tears to flow. Please do not judge yourself. Ask any painful areas in your body what it is that they want to tell you.

The answers may not come in words but in images, dreams or memories.

Next, list your positive attributes and reflect on them daily. This can be difficult for someone who habitually thinks negatively of themselves, but try to find one positive thing about yourself to add to the list every day. Each day make time to read the whole list. Take in a deep breath after each statement.

- Make your list very specific. Instead of using general adjectives to describe yourself, try listing specific actions or attributes that describe who you are and what you do.
- For example, instead of simply saying "I am generous," you can write "Any time I know that a friend is struggling, I give her a small, thoughtful gift to show that I care. This makes me generous."
- As you read and reflect on your list, remember that each item on the list, however insignificant it may seem, is a reason that you are worthy of respect and love.

Loving your suffering

I trained many years ago as a yoga teacher with one of the UK's first yoga teachers, Ruth White. Ruth was trained by Iyengar. She always told us stories of what the famous master used to tell his students. The one that stuck was this: That all suffering is of the mind. That if we can be in the present moment then there is no suffering. It is the mind and the mind alone that knows suffering.

I am far greater than the mind. When I die my mind will die. The mind identifies with the separate self. The real 'I' is connected to the universe. There is no death of the real Self.

The truth is that we suffer to the extent that we are identified with our separate self, our story, our personality, our emotions, our culture and our beliefs. It is only from this place that we tend to be jealous, envious, disconnected, unhappy, over-reactive and lacking in joy and our Shakti energy!

Can you see your story as a story? Can you see yourself as greater than your story? If you are beginning to get this, then you are on your way back home. On your way back to wholeness, love and joy. On a deeper level than you knew was possible.

Heart IQ /Heart Circling is, as I see it, is the greatest new paradigm for healing. It is neither therapy nor coaching. We sit in circle (or one on one). We do not try to 'fix' you, change you or advise you.

When in circle, we agree to step out of victim mentality and identify the role we each play in our life experiences. We agree to find out what we want in our situation and take responsibility for it. We strive to avoid stepping into the drama and getting lost in the story.

Heart Circle

There is much Love and compassion felt and experienced during a heart Circle.

Circling, or conscious communication from the heart is bigger, deeper and more than therapy. One to one or in a group this is the most powerful form of healing that I have ever come across! Circling of the heart takes one right into the centre of presence. Nothing needs 'doing.'

If you'd like to experience a heart circling event with a Heart IQ practitioner, including myself, get in touch with me on my email inspire@riseshakti.com.

Part 2

Chapter 12

Becoming More 'You'

My definition of becoming 'more you' is becoming more aligned to "who you really are".

It is important that the Goddess remembers that her way of creating is not done through strategy or logic.

The feminine Shakti energy is creative, intuitive and magnetic.

Instead of setting a goal, figuring it out, making lists and plans, start instead by connecting with the core of creative power—your deeper desires. Abraham Hicks and others talk about your desires as only being desires because you already have that which you desire in your energetic field. You just haven't aligned with it yet.

I love that!

Whereas the masculine works on the linear, the feminine is all expansive. What you are desiring, is already manifest. That is why you have such an energetic pull towards it.

How awesome is that?

So, all you need to do is let go of all structure and tap into your inner wisdom, your inner guidance system, your body mind.

What makes you feel good, siStar?

Imagine two roads. You have a choice. Which road do you choose? And would one road be the 'wrong' road if along it you learnt more about who you really are?

So gorgeous, you are now ready for this next section of the Middle -aged Goddess Playbook.

I am soooo excited for you! Are you ready? Are you ready to abandon all ideas about who you thought you were and take the very first step into the unknown world of possibility? To reconnect with that deepest part of you, your essence, your purpose on being here?

Close your eyes and take a deep breath. Allow the centre of your awareness to deepen into your body. Breathe into the centre of the most connected, wisest part of yourself, deeply taking the breath right down into the pelvis.

Imagine that you're stepping into a field of limitless possibility and that you're surrounded by a field of limitless support for the magnificent realisation of your greatest gifts and contributions!

And now from this deepest part of your awareness ask yourself these questions. Notice any thoughts or judgements that may arise.

What is my most authentic expression of who I am? In other words, what do I most deeply desire to . . .

1/Experience in my life?

2/Create in my life?

3/Express through my life?

4/Contribute to my community/friends and the world?

Breathe deeply with full awareness, and feel into the quality of sensations in your body as you answer each question, writing down what comes up for you. Notice any emotions arise when you ask these questions, asking gently and lovingly to the deepest parts of yourself. See if you can allow yourself to be touched to the core - this is the place where you can ignite your deepest desires and passions.

Say to yourself 'Please guide me to the right people, places, thoughts, situations where I may be able to more fully experience, express, create and share these deepest truths.'

Ask for guidance from the angels, from spirit or from God as to what is your next step.

Listen for the answer from that deepest part of yourself.

Trust your gut, Goddess. Trust your intuition....

And now, take action, baby! It's highly unlikely that you will have a clue what to do, think or say beyond simply taking the first step. Remember that the Goddess energy does not need a plan. However, she does require the masculine action in order to begin her creation. So, my beautiful, please do not be concerned with the how, why, where, when for now, simply take the very first step towards the next step on your beautiful evolving journey. Remember that I am here to hold your hand. And that if I can do it, then so can you!

Most people never take action because they are so afraid of failure. How seriously crazy is that? And yet it's true. What have you wanted to experience or create in your life and not pursued it for fear of failure, fear of rejection? I'm noticing in myself how long it takes for me to actually believe that I'm totally capable and worthy of doing what I do, and I notice all my limiting beliefs and negative self-talk. And I consider myself quite an expert at self-love. Completing this book has taken me years because I always made other things of greater importance! And yet, writing this book has given me the greatest joy (and healing).

In fact, writing this book has been my driving force, giving me the courage to step out and beyond all of my comfort zones, and feeling safe to share with you here in these pages. Because I know that I am another you cleverly disguised as me ....

We are one, sister!

When we learn to fully trust our deepest wisdom then miracles begin to happen.

It's like the more you let go of worry and 'what if's' then the more that the universe steps in to hold you, Mother Earth enveloping you in her loving, supporting and nurturing arms.

Can you imagine being pregnant, but not giving birth? This is how many women's lives are today. A feeling like something amazing deep inside is being created, but life just seems to get in the way of the birthing of 'it'.

So many conscious women are struggling with intimacy.

We have lived in a male dominated culture for a long time now. Power, control, science, technology, doing, making are all very masculine energies.

It is now time to access once again our Divine Goddess!

There are six areas we're going to take a look at right now because these powerful questions contain in them the very essence that we want to connect with.

Time- How much time do I have for my personal/ spiritual development?

Connection- What happened to my deepest sense of connection and what does that mean to me?

Self-expression- Am I able to express myself and who I am in the world? Do I even know who I am anymore?

What happened to my creativity? Where is she hiding? What is it that stops me creating?

What do I long for?

Where is my community? Have I found my tribe?

Goddesses, if you are to find true and lasting love, then it is absolutely essential that you reconnect with your divine feminine! You see, true love requires that you fall into love with your own true essence!

Goddess energy is receptive, soft, gentle, flowing, magnetic, intuitive. When we connect to the divine feminine we have more flow in our lives, more magic, more relatedness, ease, fluidity, connection. (Please remember that we are all men and women, made up of masculine and feminine, Yin and Yang. It's just that we got so caught up in the Yang world that we need some more balance in order to live fully authentically.)

Take out your Playbook

From each title above, write down at least 5 sentences. Whatever comes to mind. Then, take the same sentences and this time, respond to what you've written as an affirmation.

For example: Where is my TIME?

1/ I never seem to have any time to myself anymore

2/ I waste my time procrastinating,

3/ I am not inspired to make effective use of my free time

Could become:

1/ I now create some free time for ME everyday

2/ I am finding new hobbies and am planning a new business idea,

3/ I read daily positive quotes and am now exercising for 10 minutes a day.

Goddesses, I want YOU to become a more authentic version of yourself!

Take these affirmations and intentions and either stick them on the wall somewhere where you can remind yourself daily of what you have committed to do. Remember there is also a section at the end of this book to write down all of your inspirations as they begin to show up. Please do not put any pressure on yourself, but just allow the energy of the words to be absorbed into your energy field.

Collectively, soul sisters, we have the power to change the world!

Becoming more 'you' means that you don't need to try and be like someone else. When I met my Pilates teacher she appeared to me to be so 'perfect'. She had the perfect body, the perfect studio, and knew her subject and the anatomical body so much better than I did. I wanted to be like her. Because I had ulcerative colitis, at times my belly would bloat. I would also eat a lot of sugar in my otherwise 'healthy' diet of green juices! I thought I was eating healthily but I couldn't stay off the comfort food.

Coffee and a croissant (or two) was my daily treat, and in fact I realise now that it was my 'empty nest syndrome'. It really kicked in after I'd returned home from travelling for five months aged fifty-two. I got home to an empty house and realised that it was the first time really that I'd been truly alone since living in a bedsit aged nineteen! Luckily, I had a really strong group of friends, but either they had no children, or many still had teenage children at home.

There's a real loneliness that can be felt when we are faced with our own self. Friends may be able to support us, but it's rare that someone is emotionally equipped to fully hold space in which we can be heard, felt, and listened to.

How can I become more 'me' if I no longer know who 'I' am?

It saddens me immensely at how many of my sisters don't actually know who they are anymore. They wear so many hats and play so many roles that they've no idea how or whom to be. Do you recognise yourself here?

One of the best ways I have discovered to get to know yourself is by spending time alone. You can start with just a few hours, especially if you're a mum and trying to pack your life with all the duties that you've told yourself that you should be doing. The next step is to take a weekend out. Just for you. I've noticed how many excuses women make for not giving themselves this act of self-love. 'Oh, I don't have time for such luxuries!'

I believe that the real truth is that as women who have often 'ruled the roost' we have actually become addicted to the need to control. The very idea of someone else taking on the kids, cooking the meals coping better than we can, even if just for a weekend, can feel very threatening. And frightening. Because what if the woman I spend that weekend with is dull, lonely, boring, frightened and lost?

What if that woman is me?

So, beautiful Goddess....... It's a journey of courage, of self-love and appreciation, of learning the tools and then practicing, and you can take this book along with you too.

What I have learnt on my journey is that as with everything, spending time alone takes practice. Some days will be easier than others. But ultimately it is absolutely necessary if you are to get to know, to really know the most important person in your life. The one who will never leave you and will always be there for you your entire life!

Friendships

Have you asked yourself recently 'Do my friendships serve me?' We don't need to fall out with a friend in order to stop spending time with them. We all have choice and we are never 'stuck' in friendships. It is always our own beliefs and insecurities that keep us stuck in relationships that are not serving our highest good.

From facilitating circles, I know only too well how many of you literally hang on to old friends simply because they're 'old friends!' Can you be really, really honest and ask yourself if those friendships are making you feel good about yourself or bad? We tend to hang out with people in tribes, who are like ourselves. Otherwise what often happens is that we have outgrown our old friends and yet still get agitated when they annoy or upset us. My philosophy has been to be very honest with yourself and ask the following questions.

1/ Am I seeing this friend because I don't have too many other friends to choose from?

2/ What could I do with my time if I wasn't spending it with this friend?

3/ Does this friend make me feel heard, special, loved?

4/ Am I friends with this person because I feel sorry for them?

5/ Do we stay connected out of a sense of duty or loyalty?

Can you think of any other answers that might pop up, to questions I haven't yet asked?

We all want to have strong friendships. For me personally, I've always felt that on one level I have many good friends. Yet, when we move forward on our path to self, it is inevitable that we start to evolve and change. Which means that whether we like it or not, we start to have less and less in common with our old friends. Now it's natural to still want to remain friends. But it maybe that we start to spend less time with those friends. Last year I went to a Brandon Bays 3-day event in London. I was triggered in so many ways. One being that having started my Heart IQ training journey, I didn't like the way that the large audience was seated in rows facing the facilitator.

Oh, I was so judgemental beyond belief, I tried to leave on the second day and decided to exit the morning early and have my lunch in the huge conference centre's dining room. I planned my 'getaway' so that no one would know. I had prepaid my lunch and had no intention of missing out on that! So, I chose my delicious buffet and went to sit in the 'out of bounds' area of the dining space, so that when the other hundreds of attendees came out, I would not need to talk to anyone! (Yes, it's true!)

Halfway through my meal another woman came and sat with me. We have ended up not merely friends. She came to a weekend of heart circling at my place and is becoming a very deep soulmate. Not becoming, she is one!

These kinds of connections are more than friendships. The quality of these connections, once we surrender to our deepest nature, are like no other. Like a marriage based in truth, life flows, moves and grows. This fluidity of movement is by nature the feminine essence. This is our truth, siStars! This is life. Pay attention to noticing what each of your friendships brings as its gift to your soul, and notice if you feel complete. I have been very sad to make deliberate decisions not to stay connected with some very old, dear friends simply because by doing so I noticed that I left each time we met, feeling closed rather than open. I am moving towards feeling light and open constantly. Now that doesn't mean that if a friend is feeling low or depressed that I avoid her or him. It just means that if, after many years of friendship you feel that you are making leaps and bounds, and that your friend is constantly making life choices that are not in alignment with their highest truth, their highest calling, and that this is no longer fitting with your idea of how life is, then perhaps your journey spent together has had its time.

Maybe you can love from a distance. If you are constantly feeling negative after spending time with a friend, then this is not your highest truth. Remember also that our friends reflect to us where we are at (as do the men we attract- more on that later.)

See if you can spend some downtime in contemplation, a walk in nature perhaps, and ponder over your friendships. Sometimes my friendships have deepened once I've been honest with myself about the 'state' of our connection. Because usually what I am seeing in my friendships is a portal, a mirror to my own self.

When this is no longer the case, and I have evolved to a different vibration, then our connection naturally lessens and falls away, or becomes stronger, because my honesty brings up darkness to be healed for my friend too.

It can ignite a very much deeper friendship. Be open and trust your intuition. Build strong friendships where you feel valued and appreciated. Recently, a very old and dear friend of mine betrayed my trust. On deeper reflection, she was not trusting in the flow of her own life, it was nothing to do with me. I have forgiven her, but I realised that on our last skype call that I had moved on too far to connect with her anymore to the level that my soul needs. Although I love and adore her very, very much, I now need to be around people who are willing to put their lives on the line for growth. My Kali spirit is running wild and I now choose to spend time around those who want that too.

Great Goddess, I rejoice with you in all acts of pleasure and love.

What am I eating?

In the journey to becoming more of your authentic self it is important to find some support in getting healthier and more conscious food choices.

Becoming middle-aged does NOT automatically justify you being overweight, frumpy, and hiding in your baggy t shirt!

Who is the 'real' you, the woman inside who longs to be set free? Do you know that she really, really wants to be released? She craves to unravel the layers upon layers of self-doubt, of beliefs, of programming, of staying small and insignificant.

The Closer you live to the vibration of the real you, the more fulfilling your life will become ... so become fearless in your pursuit to set your soul on fire!

Although I was a Pilates teacher for over twenty years, I was never happy with my body because deep down I was able to hide my sugar addiction very well. Friends used to tell me 'you're so lucky being tall, you, can carry it.' In truth, I found that my work really helped me to stay trim, but I sure was able to hide parts that I didn't like in my tight-fitting Lycra! My sister and I would go on healthy eating marathons, drinking green juices and eating salads and homemade soups, but these would inevitably end up as croissant and biscuit fests. We jokingly blamed it on our Hungarian father's childhood of starving because he lived in one room with his aunt, who was so poor that he had to beg for food. What I have learnt on my journey is that the more I am in alignment with my true self, when I am a living embodiment of true souls' purpose and nature- that I automatically eat less, more healthily, more consciously, and my body naturally loses any excess weight that she's carrying. It's a win, win.

When I live in true alignment to my authentic self, I naturally fit my body and excess weight falls away effortlessly……

Chapter 13
Living with Presence

It's amazing how when we begin to follow our true nature, instinctively we begin to make healthier choices too.

One of the main reasons my clients give me as to why they cannot take the time to care for themselves as lovingly as they would like to, is time. Busy-ness has become the national epidemic. In fact, more than that being busy is (falsely) assumed to mean 'important'.

I have certainly suffered with this myself. After my first husband died I was lovingly known as 'busy Lizzie'. I simply never ever sat down. I darted from one thing to another, one friend's house to another's, never allowing myself time to stop.

What I was really doing was not giving myself time to feel my intense pain.

What do you do to keep yourself busy so that you don't have time to feel?

Interestingly just the other day whilst preparing to leave for my winter trip to Bali, I found myself holding and stroking my lodger's cat. I made a sudden decision to

S T O P.

I sat down (11.30am on a busy morning- how utterly alien) As I stroked the cat I caught myself saying 'don't stop now, you're mid flow getting things done, don't stop, don't stop...... and then the wiser part of me saying 'hey girl, this is exactly what you tell others to do...! Stop for 10 minutes and savour every second'

It felt as if I had stepped off the treadmill of life, and come right slap bang into the present moment. It was like taking a sneaky holiday. I felt refreshed enough to continue my tasks with a renewed sense of well-being.

Keeping ourselves busy is the national occupation. Shopping, cooking, working, seeing friends, watching TV, surfing the net, going to the gym. I hear you say, 'but those things are essential and need doing!' And I say yes, they may indeed need doing. But what is the intention?

Are you present?

Are you cooking a big meal as a duty, or could you prepare an egg salad and really savour that? And then find the time to watch the sunset?

How much have you simply just got used to 'doing stuff' to keep yourself so busy that you are numb to your actual feelings and emotional state? Are you really covering up the fact that you don't like your job, relationship, finances?

When clients new and old come to my studio, whether for heart circles, mindfulness, coaching or bodywork they always comment on how they feel as if they've 'come home'.

Being present to one's real feelings connects you to your true divine nature, which is home. It is there deep inside of you always.

Presence is always available to you, even in the midst of crisis and certainly throughout your busy day. But you must be aware of how much you are doing in relation to how often you are 'being' and then commit to make time to be less busy. And it can be done right now, you can step off the treadmill at any given moment and come into the present.

You see, the present is a gift. It is the big secret of life. When you step out of busy-ness and into presence life begins to flow. Magic will rock your world, and everything that you need comes to you effortlessly. It is just simply the mind that takes us out of presence. I see it all the time. Bring anyone into stillness of the mind and suddenly all is well. It's so simple.

This is the heart of circle work that has become my newest passion. I have never seen such instant results. Bring someone into presence, into the heart, and a whole new world comes into being. A heart centred experience of deep connection, not just to others, but to Self. To the divine. To life itself.

Now that's what I call bliss.

Take your Playbook

Divide a page into two halves. On one side write a header 'busyness' and on the other side 'Presence' Write down 5 things that you do to keep yourself busy and then offer yourself 5 alternatives that you could do to come into presence.

Here is an example:

Busy	**Present**
1) Go on Facebook	Ask myself, 'how am I feeling'?
2) Watch TV	Play my favourite music, dance
3) Shopping	Buy a Mindfulness Course
4) Making lists	Take inspired action
5) Planning weekend	No plans, just go with the flow

You really can begin to radically change the way you operate, bringing in more Shakti energy to your everyday life. It is important to recognise your current habits and coping strategies.

Some of, actually, no all my favourite experiences have been born from inspired action.

It's like the best parties. You know, the ones you go to last minute, no looking forward to it, you just arrive with no expectation and boom, you have an awesome time!

"Somewhere between what she survived, and who she was becoming, was exactly where she was meant to BE. She was starting to Love the journey. And find the comfort in the quiet corners of her wildest dreams. They say people don't change. Well, she wasn't always this way.

"Even if she didn't change the entire world, she would change her part of it. And she would affect the people she shared it with. A butterfly whose wings have been touched, can indeed still fly. Whether something was meant to be, or meant to leave, didn't matter as much anymore. She would soak up the sun, kiss the breeze and she would fly regardless."

~ J Raymond

Chapter 14
The Orgasmic Goddess

My beautiful siStar! How many courses and workshops have you attended with the dream of 'finding yourself'? Realising your life purpose? Creating your perfect life? I've done all of those things too, but what I notice is missing is the connection with our bodies.

The majority of the women that I work with where I live in a middle-class cathedral city just outside of North London, are simply not *embodied*. Now if we are to enjoy intimacy with another we must be able to create intimacy with self. We need to experience a far greater capacity for pleasure than we know is possible!

Sadly, too many middle-aged women who are in relationships have lost the magic that they might have once experienced with their partner. What shocks me more is how many younger women have never even experienced the magical bliss that can be experienced from being fully embodied, usually through a deeply held dislike of their body.

That certainly was me too.

We need to come into contact with our most incredible gift that we have as a human being...... our body!

We are living in a time of severe disconnect. For many, the very words 'self-pleasure' may conjure up emotions of disgust, shame or denial. There may be a whole host of reasons for this, and in later chapters I talk more about the subject of shame and also the history of how the church made us 'wrong' for having sensual connection to our bodies. Sinful thoughts of our bodies and pleasure were deemed as wrong, and we must repent and ask for forgiveness. No wonder we've all grown up with distorted ideas around our sexuality!

Even with all the progress we have made as women, there is still one significant area that absolutely needs addressing if we are to fully awaken. We are cut off from our sexuality and therefore our pleasure and our power.

I have seen many amazing, conscious women full of knowledge, experience and wisdom, with the intention of living a vibrant authentic life and yet still being deeply unhappy, hungry for something 'more' that they just can't quite touch.

We are awakening to our divine feminine and yet something extraordinarily essential is missing!

Unless we integrate our sexuality as part of our awakening on our spiritual journey then we will always be fragmented...

If we seriously want to become more conscious then we cannot leave our bodies out of the equation.

And it's easy for us to touch deep states of pleasure and even ecstasy. We simply have not had access to the tools because there is so much shame around this in our culture.

SiStar- it's time to reclaim our bodies. This awareness is not only delicious and juicy ~ it is essential to our awakening!

Your sexual energy can be channelled into all that you do, from having a great business idea to playing with your grandchildren. From finding your playfulness to creating your perfect life. The orgasmic Goddess resides inside every woman, waiting to be unleashed!

We all know the story of the wicked step mother or the young heroine, and these different personalities, or archetypes can be reflected, so that we can see various aspects within ourselves.

The goddess of sacred sex invites us to open to the sacred and to be aware that love-making is a gateway that can connect us with the divine.

Lilith is the dark goddess of the Hebrew faith the Kabbalah, a seductress, as far back as 4000 BC, in the Sumerian culture. She would bring men from the streets to the temple prostitutes (I talk more about this later)

Today she represents a modern archetype of female sexual empowerment, the seductress and the wild woman! Sisters, it's now time to explore the shadow to see what it holds and how we can heal the long-standing wounded feminine. Female sexuality has long been denied through the patriarchal religions which sadly caused a split - one which has existed between the sexes since the rise of patriarchy.

Without awakening and integrating our sexuality into our spiritual journey, we will always be fragmented...

Our bodies seem to get left out of the equation when it comes to becoming more conscious. I have seen so many beautiful women touch the depths of their soul through embodied movement. Conscious movement is becoming more and more popular through practices such as ecstatic dance and 5Rythms.

I believe that it is the shame that we carry with us constantly that denies us access to our true abundance of raw powerful, creative sexual energy! It has been distorted and manipulated through patriarchal societies to be 'dirty' 'embarrassing' and 'cheap' if we are to fully express our shakti sacred sexual Goddess. The shadow has been pornography, secret sex, scandal, lying, cheating, infidelity, escorts, sex addiction, fetishes, sexual dysfunction, self-loathing and much more.

But sex is a natural act, a loving expression shared between two individuals, for the purpose of pleasure and procreation. It is an opportunity to merge energies and come together to meet another, physically, mentally, emotionally and spiritually. Everything is an act of sex. The union of the energies merging with each other to give rise or birth to new experiences, from the creation of universes to flowers and trees, to a cake being made, to a piece of music or art being made or performed. Sex should be honoured and revered for the divine expression that it is. But with the creation of duality, what arose was the shadow side of sex. We went into hiding parts of our sexual selves from others and even ourselves. The denial and repression of aspects of the self, fed the shadow, giving it a life of its own.

Sexual energy is so powerful that it's vital that we become conscious of it or we drop into the shadow. Sex is not shameful and yet, we've been fed so much shame that the shadow side in our society is like a cancer.

It's time to heal the shadow!

We should never feel anger, regret or shame for our sexual actions and it is our cultural programming that seems to have the upper hand in pushing us towards shame over pleasure and lust over real and intimate loving connections.

Everything is connected to one's level of consciousness. The more consciousness one brings to their experiences, the deeper and more profound the experiences can be. Just as with the shadow, sex can be quite a destructive force, its potential for being a profoundly healing, regenerative and transformative experience is massive.

We also need to honour the sacredness of The Sex Act- accepting and healing the Shadow within us, learning from it, not judging it, embracing and forgiving whatever gave rise to such experiences or energies, and choosing to release it in Love, as we step into our wholeness and express that wholeness in every area of our life- the workplace, the community, the world, and of course the bedroom.

Sexuality gets little mention in the sacred texts of Judaism, Islam, and Christianity. When it is mentioned, the suggestion is often to avoid it if possible in order to reach greater spiritual heights. Many monks and gurus also teach that we must refrain from sex to reach enlightenment.

Yet none of us would be here without sex. There is virtually no spiritual instruction in how to deal with sexual urges other than to abstain. As a result, many people experience a split between sexuality and spirituality in their lives.

Since I discovered five rhythms and ecstatic dance I have felt much more accepted in my feminine essence, as if I've been allowed to be sexy and feminine. Much of the spiritual work, particularly the heart circle and heart IQ work and the rise of the sisterhood groups have helped me to realise that my abundance of sexuality is natural and not the shameful dark shadow that I used to believe it to be.

And my research for this book has been pretty mind blowing too!

Take your Playbook

Write down any thoughts that have arisen for you. Allow your pen to flow freely.

I invite you to download my 'Middle aged Goddess workout' and experience for yourself how liberating it can feel to dance. Imagine that you're in a room full of other sisters, and let yourself drop into the music, move from that place....

Allow yourself to get in touch with your Shakti

She awaits....

Welcome the wild Goddess!

A wild Goddess cares deeply for her temple.

She knows that her body is the earthly manifestation of her spiritual and emotional self.

She eats consciously, choosing fresh, organic wholefoods, fruits and vegetables. She practises mindful conscious embodied exercise such as Pilates, Yoga or Tai chi, and she enjoys creative ecstatic dance practices such as five rhythms, because this wild Goddess absolutely loves to dance!

She rests when she needs to, and understands the importance of taking care of her body and her body's needs.

When she attends to the emotional, mental, physical and spiritual aspects then her body easily maintains its natural weight.

And most of all, a wild Goddess feels good in her body and moves with confidence, power and grace.

What can you do right now to take one small step to becoming that Goddess? Can you picture her in your mind's eye? Close your eyes. Can you see yourself as the healthiest, most vibrant expression of who you really are?

Have you shut down your sexual body from fear of being hurt, shamed, rejected, or from self-loathing?

Take your Playbook

Please write a list NOW of activities that would bring you more into your body. Your inner Goddess is starting to stir, and if you cannot yet feel her, think of some activities that you could do to begin to stir her.

Examples are: Join a class or an online tribe for support

Cut out sugars

Cut out caffeine

Practice deep breathing

Bolster fat-busting (to break down unwanted toxins in the body)

Find a beginners Tantra workshop

Explore sacred sexuality

Read this book again and again

Remember how good it feels to orgasm!

What else could you think of doing that would support you in becoming that earthly, sexy, grounded, healthy, beautiful Goddess that you really are?

I've just attended the very first 'Awaken the Goddess' festival in London. In fact, I was invited to be the keynote speaker (the law of attraction was at work big time - as I only phoned up to enquire about getting a stall!)

I also took part in my beautiful friend Shakti Sundari's 'Dancing the Goddess' performance and then a workshop that she facilitated in the afternoon. I was literally shocked to my core as well as deeply saddened by the remarks that many of the women present made about menopause. Several believed that orgasm wasn't possible, that a woman's body didn't really enjoy sex anymore and that she lost interest anyway once her menopause began.

I assured these awakening Goddesses that it was completely and totally untrue, and that my own orgasms and self-pleasuring were the richest and most delicious experiences of my life. Even though I have had some amazing lovers. Although I've been single for many years now, it's going to take some awesome Shiva to match my own level of orgasmic delight!

Body Image

I have yet to meet a woman who is happy with her body. Most who are stick thin, look old and haggard, so I try not to refer to healthy as necessarily 'thin'.

However, when a healthy diet/eating regime is adhered to, then the body naturally finds it's ideal weight. Extra pounds will fall away and with the right exercise the body will become strong and toned. Sometimes Goddesses carry extra weight because they have a layer of protection that has manifested as weight.

SiStar... have you battled with self-hatred?

We are faced in our daily lives with images of how a woman's body should look. The models in the magazines and the mannequins in the clothes' shops are just not a true reflection of our real bodies. No wonder we have so many body issues! When I was in Finsbury Park last week heading to a dance practice I noticed that the models in the shops there, had big bums and large thighs - by large I mean about 5 times bigger than the usual mannequins! It felt reassuring and real.

Perhaps you're even feeling unlovable because you are underweight, or have stretch marks.

I was covered in acne and scarring and that always affected my self-esteem more than anyone could imagine.

What affected your self-esteem?

Our self-image issues affect every single area of our lives. But especially when it comes to orgasm.

To be liberated and free one must abandon all issues of low self-esteem and poor body image.

I remember looking in the mirror and deciding this was not the woman I had planned on becoming and that I needed to take drastic action. I didn't know how long it was going to take, but I was absolutely certain that I was going to find self-love and to start becoming the woman that I knew I was, deep inside. You know, the one who looks good, loves deeply, lives from her passion and enjoys her life.

Perhaps you know your version of this woman and perhaps you've yet to meet her. But she's real and she awaits you. I've written this book to help you (and me) claim our truest version of who we really are. (Warts n' all but a more authentic version than the current one.)

My whole life became a quest for health, to give up my nicotine addiction, to heal from grief and to free myself from dis-ease. And of course, I was going to share and teach my journey along the way so that I could feel some value and worthiness.

This was the underlying reason that I started to travel. I felt that I could find solace and support from the sunshine, the ocean and free myself from the binds of daily routine. My soul was calling for me to take some drastic action and I honoured that calling.

In my world, sharing is caring, and even if only one person tells me that I inspired them to change their own life, then I feel that it will have been worth it.

As I said earlier, in my work it always surprises me to hear from so many women who have never or rarely experienced orgasm. A woman shuts down, contracts and closes when she is not fully received.

Energetically we take on from our mother, our grandmother and all our ancestors. We have been repressed as women. Taught that sex is dirty, that we should not masturbate, that we are 'cheap', and that sex is wrong.

We have deeply embedded patterns of rejection and insecurity which dictate the way in which we feel about ourselves. And as for religion, the male dominated dogmatic views of the church and other women which have repressed us beyond measure. Is it no wonder that so many women cannot reach climax!

Women today are done with the Christian model of femininity that they have been brainwashed with since little girls, Sex was never spoken about in my house and the very idea of a sexy woman's body immediately tuned me in to the energy of deep shame! My father used to hide his pornographic magazines in his work case and my sister and I would go to the case and look at images of voluptuous maidens spreading their legs and pouting their lips. We were only around 8 years old and we felt very, very naughty!

What did you do as a child that felt naughty sexually and gave you a profound sense of shame afterwards?

I wonder if you could write that down now as an adult, without the bondage of guilt and repression taught to you by your mother and your mother's mother. It is not their fault. They were brainwashed.

It is once again safe, as it was in times gone by, for women to access the full power and spectrum of their sexuality, exploring the shadow without the attachment of shame. And siStar, by doing this, we are helping to heal the wounded feminine, for she has been crying out for this for millennia.

Can you believe that in the old day's words that once meant Priestess and Fertile (Ora and Halle) were given new names of 'whore'?!

The original Sex Goddess was Lilith.

In ancient times she was the dark deity but today she is the archetype of female sexual empowerment .The seductress and the wild woman who has freedom, independence and refuses to be subordinated to men. Lilith has thrown off the sacred whore label and is honoured nowadays by women the world over as the sex Goddess! You can learn more about Lilith in my chapter on the seven Goddess archetypes.

It is now time to reawaken our sexual desires!

A good friend of mine, and world renowned inspirational teacher of Women's sacred sexuality, Anaiya Sophia, shares some wonderful insights on her website, AnaiyaSophia.com on this subject of the sacred whore, and much more besides.

By celebrating our very own sacredness we cannot deny our potent sexuality. It is time for the middle-aged Goddess to finally cast off the shackles and explore the true meaning of intimacy, because intimacy without connecting to this potent energy is like a doughnut without the jam....

Well perhaps not.

But you get me, siStar

When was the last time you self-pleasured? Whether single or in a relationship unless your partner is always available (and I would hope that he is not) my thoughts are that for the ultimate experience of life Self-pleasure is one of the juiciest and most orgasmic experiences a human being can experience.

Until you know and experience what really turns you on to the point of divine orgasmic experience then I believe you are not living the full human experience. Have you ever reached such a heightened state that you become one with all that is? Have you?

In 2013, whilst living in Bali I made time to discover the most authentic version of self-pleasure. I no longer needed to imagine another with me, I was simply in union with the divine. This experience gave me a richness to my life that I had not imagined possible. I had experienced some amazing incredible lovers in my time. But this was different.

I often suggest to women who have problems with orgasm to try a few of the following. If you do orgasm, I'd like to suggest that it is possible to have a deeper and more connected experience.

Take an afternoon or evening or just even an hour out for a date with yourself. Remember that unless you can experience this alone then you will not achieve such a high state with another. This is not about sex, pornography or utilisation. This is about connecting to the deepest wisdom of the being. This is who you really are.

Have you taken time to know what turns you on?

Perhaps silk sheets, massage, sensual oils, atmospheric music. Know yourself. Enjoy touch and sensation. Notice judgements, criticism, old beliefs that might be stopping you from fully experiencing.

When I was in my early thirties the amount I had drunk would then depend on how daring I could be with my husband. I remember so wishing I was carefree. But the only way to be carefree was through drink and drugs.

For me, living in a hot climate where the skin is experienced and a light sheet on a naked body is all that is required does remind me often of the pleasures available.

So many women have been so programmed into shame around their sexual energy. I see it every day. It's not spoken about and I believe it's in epidemic proportions!

I've discovered how many siStars there are who have never experienced an orgasm. It's a problem that many women have confided in me, so I guess there are many more who would not dare to talk about such an intimate subject. This saddens me so much, because orgasm is one of the most.... No, THE most erotic, sensual, delicious, relaxing, energising, ecstatic, juicy experiences known to a Goddess.

Do you believe that you can become the Goddess of orgasm? And did I tell you......We always become what we believe.

Take out your Playbook

Write down a minimum of five things you are going to do to reignite the orgasmic Goddess within you.

I have been single now pretty much for seven years and in that time I've discovered that I can find happiness, peace and amazing, delicious, mind blowing orgasms regularly.

I try to make a point of self-pleasuring as often as possible, and with practices of self-love and teachings in this book I believe that it's possible. It is the mind that prevents orgasm and the mind can be changed.

As I write this particular paragraph I am teaching on a retreat in Portugal with my good friend, and fellow women's facilitator, Shakti Sundari. Most of the participants here are my Pilates clients and they do not want to join us in any of the heart Circling or (gentle) tantric practices. And yet as the week has gone on, we have been subtly introducing practices through breathwork, kundalini yoga, and deep relaxation to nourish mind, body and soul. Many of the women are in their late fifties, as I am, and have been married for around thirty years. I'd be very curious to know how their sex life has changed on returning home this coming week, given the amount of beautiful embodied practices we've done, but of course I won't be asking!

Unless an avid 'hippy' many women of my era and bought up in middle class England have been sexually repressed. Either that, or the shadow of swinging parties and affairs has become the outlet.

The most natural and healthy expression of this energy is to tap into it without shame and repression.

Other practices could be to dance sensually and seductively, practice slow deep breath work with sound (try making the sound of having an orgasm) or self-massage - inner thighs, belly, breasts etc. There are some super deliriously fragrant oils on the market, Ylang Ylang is just one aromatherapy oil that can induce your sensuality.

Notice any beliefs, judgements, criticism that try to dissuade and interrupt your natural desires and pleasures. Remember to breathe deeply to help you to relax.

Do you have an old (or recent) photo of yourself that you could stick on your fridge? One with the body that you desire, and perhaps another of you looking gorgeous and sexy, perhaps all rolled into one photo even? If not, then find a picture of someone with a similar body type and stick that on your fridge instead. Perhaps also if you struggle with relating to your sexy orgasmic Goddess, then stick up a picture of a woman who you would like to look like. Every time you go to the fridge for a sneaky peep, take a good long look at the photo. Tell yourself that there is a wild, sexy, orgasmic Goddess within you, waiting to be unleashed! She is so welcome to be part of your life. She misses being allowed to show up- more often than you've probably given her permission to. And she longs to express herself.

Chapter 15
What is Tantra?

Tantra in the west is often misconstrued as being 'all about sex' and this grates on me. Why? Because in truth, Tantra has nothing to do with sexuality- and yet it has everything to do with it. But when we focus on the sexual side only (which is only a really tiny minute part of Tantra) then I believe that the ancient truths of Tantra are lost. It is a system, a philosophy and technology so intuitive and natural to man that its essence can be seen within all genuine spiritual paths, from Taoism, Tibetan Buddhism, Kabbalah and Tarot, to the cults of the Ancient Egyptians and even within Christianity.

Energy and consciousness

In Tantra, Consciousness is known as Shiva, and energy is Shakti. The manifest and the un-manifest.

Shiva is therefore pure, un-manifested latency without form or shape. According to the Tantric philosophy, thought, matter and everything we can perceive through the five senses, including the electrical currents that we feel moving through our bodies, is a love-dance of Shiva and Shakti.

Tantra is a life embracing, celebratory philosophy that includes all of creation and the Tantric practices likewise embrace all of life.

Tantra is different to our modern model of relationship and intimacy.

It's about energetic connection, and not just the physical pleasure that we've grown to understand in our culture of throw away instant gratification. Not to say that you cannot have one night of pure ecstatic bliss in a tantric connection. But it's the energy of it that's different.

The Tantra model is a way of merging between two souls with no goals to reach, whereas the modern sex and relationships look for an outcome like climax or satisfaction.

Tantra considers the external reality to be a manifestation of your internal, and so a tantric relationship is as much a journey to your own soul as it is to the soul of your partner. As Marianne Williamson says, so beautifully in her book 'Enchanted Love'

"What ultimately attracts both men and women is the fire of initiation, the unconscious lure of the situation that represents the next stage of our personal growth."

But the only way we can teach others is by conscientiously trying to learn our own lessons in their presence.

To me, this is what Tantra is all about. This is what I long for. At the ripe age of 56 as I write this chapter (I only seem to be able to write these words when I'm in Bali, hence this book is taking a loooong time to complete!) I really will never again be able to go into an unconscious relationship on any level. I have made a commitment to myself. I'd rather be alone than return to the drama of being in a relationship with someone who is not absolutely willing to be, and grow into the fullest and most authentic version of their true Self. I have many friends in the 'Tantra' and sacred sex worlds, so I'm constantly seeing posts on Facebook asking about what others want sexually, or what brings them the most pleasure, or how they can get more sex and sex, sex, sex, sex....

And I'm thinking... has anyone else just, gotten over it?? Do they really think it's all about sex?

Tantra goes beyond everything that our past experiences, our society, our culture and our religions have conditioned us to believe about sex and relationships

Tantra can have ripple effects on every other aspect of your life — your finances, career, life purpose, health, family, spirituality, and more. Our sexual energy is the most incredible, yet underused source of evolutionary power that we have. Our erotic energy is a divine intelligence that when we learn to circulate it through our body it literally lights up our lives, enlivening positive qualities and awakening archetypal soul aspects of ourselves, we never even knew existed. We might have touched on some of these energies over the years, and in various relationships, but then dismissed them through negative judgements and shame.

When we reclaim our Shakti as a sovereign source, it can make huge shifts in our lives.

Physically we can go from feeling flat and tired, to feeling vital, alive and energised. Creatively we can go from feeling lost and directionless to feeling inspired and on fire. On a mental level we can go from feeling dull, foggy and 'all over the place' to feeling clear and aligned. Emotionally we can go from feeling shut down and closed to feeling open, warm and loving. Spiritually we can go from feeling lost and disconnected to feeling ecstatically joyful and connected to the Divine.

Why or how could we want anything else?

I am new to Tantra and it feels like this part of me has been lying dormant my whole life. Like it was there, but not fully expressed. Shame, conditioning, grief, lack of self-love, everyday living, raising a family in the '80's, trauma and being a business owner, all kept me trapped in a system that didn't allow my full expression as a woman.

Taking on 'Shakti' as part of my name was taking on a huge commitment and trust that I could somehow step into the shoes of the divine Goddess. My mind questioned it, but I knew that I had to do it. I hardly even knew what Shakti meant. And now I am in absolute awe of this life because as I was writing the previous sentence; a white feather stroked my shoulder and fell onto my laptop. This has never happened before.

It feels like a message from the Angels

I am finally allowing my true nature to emerge.

As I become more involved, evolved and embodied I am finding that my pull towards tantra is growling naturally. It was never a subject that I wanted to have forced upon me, especially after meeting many self-proclaimed 'Tantric teachers' generally male and often taking advantage of their female customers. One teacher, whom I've discovered recently on social media is Tanja Diamond.

I asked Tanja to say something about her lineage and tantra teachings and she had this to say:

"True Tantra has been left in the dust in the west. Instead of encompassing the power of transformation, it has been turned into a sex driven feel good spiritual bypass experience of little substance. Losing all its actual power.

As Lineage Tantra holder I carry the wisdom and knowledge of my Guru and all his teachers from the beginning of the lineage. When I work with students I teach the foundations of energy mastery, how to become integrated which then brings them into a real integrity from which they can begin to attain personal freedom.

Neo/Western Tantra is little to do with Tantra and is a hybrid of eastern sex arts and new age spirituality. It focuses on sexual arousal and bigger better orgasms and love and light. We do need sexual healing in a repressed society, although we need it from credible, safe and knowledgeable people.

In society today we have so many things people are appropriating the word Tantra for. In truth, there is Lineage Tantra handed down from Guru to student in an unbroken energetic transmission, classical Tantra what we read about in Sanskrit scripture which branches off into different schools, countries and paths. Then the Western dilutions and made up practices without the solid foundations. Things called Pink Tantra, Shaman Tantra, Green Tantra, Hooker Tantra and much more haunt the lineage holders and masters of the world's most powerful technology for human transformation and salvation."

Chapter 16
Women and Shame

Brene Brown researched this huge subject and came up with this definition of shame.

Shame is the intensely painful feeling or experience of believing we are flawed and therefore unworthy of acceptance and belonging. Women often experience shame when they are entangled in a web of layered, conflicting and competing social-community expectations. Shame leaves women feeling trapped, powerless and isolated.

I believe that the single biggest issue around shame that women have is their body. I have had my fair share of shame around body image. When I was I was fourteen I returned home from my first holiday abroad in Hungary with my parents. I was chosen for the netball team and on the first day back at school I remember putting on my gym slip and noticing that I suddenly had thighs. And I didn't like them.

I spent my teenage years wishing I had a boy's body. And as for the acne! Every time I looked in the mirror, whether at home or at school I would feel so incredibly unlucky. Big red spots completely covered a pretty face. I felt so much shame, despair and embarrassment. To make things worse, after always being quite popular with the boys until the age of 10, a boy in my year 2 class told me I had a face like a pancake! I laugh now as I write this. But for a girl entering womanhood these kinds of cruel comments can be devastating!

I am sure that every Goddess reading this will have her own story to tell of torment, ridicule and bullying. What is yours? How has it affected your life?

So, throughout my teenage years I was very self-conscious and then when I married at 22, my husband and I were both so embarrassed by our bodies that we hardly ever caught sight of each other naked! Now if you are from a liberal minded family and upbringing you're probably thinking 'what the f***!' But trust me, I was so shamed that I would go to great lengths to hide my naked body.

A friend recently told me how she and others ran naked through a forest. I so want to do that!

Brene Brown goes on to say from her studies that these social-community expectations and the way they are enforced by the people in our lives are, in turn, constantly reinforced by a very powerful media culture. The media culture is what we see on television, in advertising and marketing. It's what we see in movies, what we hear in music and what we read in newspapers and magazines.

What makes shame so powerful is its ability to make us feel trapped, powerless and isolated. What makes it so dangerous is its ability to make us feel as if we are the only one— different— on the outside of the group. Many of us fall prey to the same sources of shame as other women, and we experience very similar reactions.

However, due to the isolating and secretive nature of shame, we feel as if it is only happening to us and that we must hide it at all costs.

Shame demands that we hide our 'shamed selves' from others to avoid additional shame. But I've learned that when you look at shame and shame-making experiences in a social context, something amazing happens— shame turns into collective vulnerability and people realise that they are not alone.

In further chapters of this Playbook I shall be weaving in and out of ancient wisdoms, archetypes, Goddesses and traditions. The whole Goddess 'thing' was not part of my understanding nor my language either, which a few years ago I found to be too *airy fairy.*

After I made the decision to take on my name 'Shakti' I began to allow her to flow through me. Sometimes it was hard. Sometimes I felt like a fake. Seeing beautiful women around the world taking on this huge name in honour of the divine feminine, speaking in a language that almost felt foreign to me at times. In a way, I've had to finally surrender to allow 'her' truth to come forth.

Even as I write these words, I feel the vibration and energy of something so magnificent that I find myself grasping for new words. I am noticing more and more that as I open myself to new experiences, greater awareness and higher states, that I'm searching for new ways of describing my state too. There is such a delicate refinement that is happening, piece by piece, like a jigsaw puzzle. I am just being guided, going with the flow, and listening to my intuition.

There is nothing quite like the feeling of writing down the experience of being tuned into this magical energy! To the astonishing light of my own being.

And it's in you too. She is there, waiting to be released. That gorgeous, harmonious, sexy, loving, delicate, tender, adorable aspect of you sister. Let's walk hand in hand.

The 'me too' campaign recently which has become viral on social media is an excellent example of what's starting to happen as more and more women release themselves from hiding in shame around sexual abuse. I also wrote a post of how my late first husband was sexually abused by a priest. It happens to men too, granted not as often, but it happens. Sadly, some of my blood relatives felt shame around my open postings, but I realised that if I were to keep my mouth shut then I would just be supporting the same shame energy that I write about so passionately in these pages.

I see truth as the only way forward if we are to move into a better world for our children's children. I forgive ignorance but being shamed for believing in, and supporting our collective healing does sadden me, especially when coming from my own flesh and blood. And yet I fully forgive because they are not as exposed to as many people and open-hearted sharing as I am, and so to them this is still shameful and private. It is their conditioning.

As my good friend, author, facilitator and priestess Shakti Sundari wrote recently on the subject

"One of the things that happens to those that are abused is that they feel guilty and ashamed. This, along with fear of reprisal or judgement, as well as the normalisation of sexist behaviour, often encourages those affected by abuse to stay silent. This is how the powerful stay in power. That is how all oppressive political systems survive. Insidious programming and a culture of FEAR'. One of the great things about the #metoo campaign is that the silenced are finding a voice."

Another friend wrote, "I celebrate the truth. I have been talking about this in Australia in an environment dominated by rough comments and remarks from males (presented as jokes or friendship), grabbing and rubbing included, and with women that consent to this by turning it into a laugh or a joke or just answering back with similar behaviour at the Cairns Cruising Yacht Squadron. (I wish I could tag it just to plant the seed). I wouldn't mind if some of the roughest characters could see your post Shakti Kali... For them it is normal I understand. It was heavy for me. That was one of the big reasons why I moved. It was a corrosive environment for me in that sense. And I don't even mention the reactions I got when I disapproved of those things. Attacked from all ways under the Australian flag calling it 'Australian Culture'"

You speak up Shakti Kali Kaloczi. #MeToo the ones that are not willing to recognise this truth will of course disapprove and undermine the subject. There is hope that some seed is planted.

Take your Playbook

Write down all the experiences about which you might still feel some shame in your life. Have you been abused? Open to the lessons from these difficult times and explore how you might transform your shame into wisdom. Consider even sharing these stories with trusted friends and seeking their support as a way of shifting towards love and empowerment.

Chapter 17
The Crone Goddess

It's time to reclaim the wise woman of ancient times!

The concept of crone existed tens of thousands of years ago when women's lives were seen in three stages — Maiden, Mother, and Crone. The Maiden was the youthful, independent woman. The Mother was a woman who guided others–as a biological mother or as a teacher. The Crone was the postmenopausal woman who enjoyed a special, revered status.

The old hag at her cauldron is perhaps the usual image of the Wise Woman and at a time when women were the healers of their communities. They were shamans, witches, midwives, medicine women, and priestesses of the Goddess

The Crone is a symbol of inherent wisdom that comes from experience.

She has lived through love, sorrow, hope, and fear, coming out of it all a wise and confident spirit. Through these experiences she has learned the secrets of life and death and of the mysteries beyond this world.

She has tasted death itself and watched those she loved, make the journey before her. It is through her mourning that she faces death, grows to understand it, and becomes the gatekeeper between worlds.

The wisdom of the Crone comes only after learning the lessons of non-judgment and compassion. Through these lessons the Crone becomes the balancing scales between light and dark and between life and death. She is selfless, yet she loves herself. She is kind, yet she knows when to be harsh. She is free, she is compassionate, and she is wise.

The Crone is full of power. Her body is no longer fertile, but her mind is completely able to express wisely, with compassion and understanding. She no longer bleeds, keeping her power within her and owning it without shame or fear.

She is often seen as a healer, working in tune with nature to cure ailments and guide those ready to leave or enter this world. The Crone now has her own thoughts and experiences to guide her and doesn't rely on others to decide what she will do with her life.

The Goddess is within each of us.

Listen to your inner wisdom and walk a path that nourishes your spirit.

Jean Shinoda Bolen has written two books explaining the connection between women today and the ancient goddesses. She explains that according to Jungian psychology "*women are influenced by powerful inner forces, or archetypes, which can be personified by ... goddesses.*"

These attributes live on today in the collective unconscious as an archetype. An archetype is a pattern of instinctual behaviour that is contained in the collective unconscious - a part of the unconscious mind - that is not individual but universal, with contents and modes of behaviour that are more or less the same in all cultures and in all individuals. (More on archetypes in the following chapter.)

The Crone Goddess represents the archetype of the older woman.

When patriarchy became the dominant mode, when the divine was depicted solely as male, and as women became second-class citizens, the ideas about goddesses and the archetypes they represented went underground.

Women today are reclaiming their power; these archetypes are re-emerging. Women are coming into their own as individuals, stronger and more comfortable with who they are. Crone, hag, and witch used to be positive words for old women.

As I explained in the introduction to this book (and am repeating because I feel that this information needs repeating) crone comes from crown, indicating wisdom emanating from the head; hag comes from hagio meaning holy; and witch, comes from wit meaning wise. Crones, hags, and witches which frequently were leaders, midwives and healers in their communities.

The meanings of these three words, however, were distorted and eventually reversed during the 300 years of the Inquisition when the male-dominated church wanted to eliminate women holding positions of power. Women identified as witches, who were often older women, i.e. crones and hags, were tortured and burned, and the words witch, crone, and hag took on the negative connotations that continue in our language. In the early 1980's the crone became popularised again and women started to recognise the power of the crone for her wisdom and what she has to offer the world.

Menopause can be a very emotional and exhausting time of life and comes to the Goddess often before the crone years.

But first a little something on menstruation, or 'moon cycle' as she's often known as.......

The moon is the feminine energy and represents the mother and the receptive principle.

In ancient times there were thirteen 'moonths' in a year, since there are thirteen full moons in a year and therefore thirteen menstrual cycles annually.

The thirteenth letter of the alphabet is a letter 'M' and associated with many things feminine, including mother, mama, mammary glands, menstruation and one of the most powerful feminine archetypes in the world, the Virgin Mary.

Friday the 13th was originally a day of honouring the Sacred Feminine Cycle and the creational energy of rebirth.

Friday is the day of Venus; the goddess of feminine love and women's cycles are ruled by the moon - in a year there are 13 moons and 13 women's cycles. Friday 13th was a day of celebrating, honouring and connecting with the deep feminine wisdom of death, rebirth, and creation.

Like so much of the Feminine story, the sacred ceremonies of this day were corrupted, twisted and vandalised into something that we fear, causing us to shrink away from honouring our cycle, causing us to forget our feminine rituals and the wisdom of the womb. It is time for the feminine to remember her ancient inner wisdom, it is time for her to remember the old ways and rise in her divinity. It is time for the collective feminine to reclaim her boundaries, resurrect the forgotten rituals of connection and rebirth into the power of her divine and natural love.

Goddess ... if you have stopped bleeding then your cycle is that of the midnight Goddess - New moon to New Moon!

Welcome to the blessing of menopause!

My life changed for the better after menopause and it makes me sad to see some of my sisters grieve for a time that they will never get back.

Now is the time to call upon the Crone Goddesses who are wonderful at helping you deal with the menopause, or the changes happening to your body and emotions or to help face your own mortality.

She can help you remember the cycles of life if you are experiencing a loss. Invoke the crone Goddesses to help you face your deepest fears. The Crones encourage you dear siStar to be wild and free, for they show us the strength and courage that lies within us all.

When you're in the flow of your beautiful potent menopausal and postmenopausal energy, you're tapping into something so ancient, something innate to all women.

Sweetheart, when the Goddess in you arrives at this phase of our life we become the one others turn to for advice and comfort. Woven throughout this book has been the message of love, wisdom and compassion that becomes the way of the crone, for we have experienced life. Oh boy, have we?!

I went through my menopause in my mid-forties, without any complication. One theory by one of the 'Harley St. specialists' who incidentally are some of my friends, was that my body was so intrinsically unhealthy that it just stopped menstruating.

I was never ever in the flow, nor did I align with any 'moon cycle.' Having random periods when my emotionally battered body felt like it, roughly every 3 or 4 or 5 weeks was typical of my chaotic life. My periods were excruciatingly heavy in my thirties. The final straw came one day when I literally dropped my huge clots of blood into a carrier bag in my bedroom. It was like giving birth to twins. I went to my GP; the experience of a moon cycle was feeling like a death cycle (ah...... as I write this I see the wisdom here.......) and so I opted for a new product on the market, the Marina Coil. This would end my periods for good. What a fucking relief!

However, in those days of ignorance I didn't know nor understand what I do now. We have given away our power to patriarchal ideologies, taken drugs to stop our bleeding, used cancer causing chemically bleached tampons to stop the flow, called it 'the curse!

It really is time sisters to reclaim the honouring of the sacred regenerative 'flowering' of our wombs and rejoice!

Goddess Kali represents female power, wrath, and the psychic force of menstruation. Menstruation is indeed deeply connected to the cycles of time; it represents the cyclic force of destruction that precedes fertility. Life is an ever-flowing cycle of death and rebirth. This is the reason that, so many Hindu and Tibetan goddesses feature the colour red in their images.

Everything in nature flows in cycles.

Take your Playbook

Start to write about how you feel about your menopause. Have you begun yet? Did it arrive early, late? Is there fear, joy, concern, symptoms, agitation?

Treat this as a journaling exercise and allow the pen to flow. Get in touch with your true feelings around this phase of your journey. Feel into any worries, doubts, sadness.

Perhaps you wanted children and it didn't happen. Can you feel the pain of your grief? Breathe into all emotions and allow the wise part of you to comfort the part that feels any loss, regret or pain. I seem to be standing alone in that I simply sailed through menopause. It never concerned me emotionally. I couldn't wait.

How much this affected my lack of symptoms I am not sure. But what I do know is that all my female friends and clients go through a pretty rough ride. Somehow, I missed out on the regularity of moon cycles, the loving kindness to my body as an appreciation of her womanhood. Whatever the reason for my lack of menopausal symptoms, I feel very grateful that I was spared the misery of what so many of my peers are going through!

I really don't know how much my hormones combined with my attitude, my refusal to grow old gracefully, my health and perhaps pure luck meant that I didn't suffer one little bit during menopause. But remember, to all my dear sweaty sisters....

This too shall pass....

Chapter 18
The Goddess of Transformation

It's time for me to now properly introduce you to Kali. Kali is a very powerful goddess. In India she is one of the most beloved of all the Goddesses. She is known often as the dark goddess who governs time, death, and transformation.

Kali is not afraid of your darkness. She will show you that the mask that you wear is not the real you. In fact, she will help you to realise that your power is weakened by all the pretence. It weakens you because it uproots you from the totality of who you are.

"Come," she says, "I will take you into the darkest of the dark, into the places of regret and shame, into the most vulnerable corners of your being, and I will show you that all which you feared would break you, are portals to your greatness."

~Chameli Devi Ardagh

Kali often arrives in times of crisis, when your perspective is turned upside down: illness, breakups, redundancy, career change, you know those times when it feels like your entire world is falling apart. She evokes transformation from within, standing for radical honesty and radical freedom from false attachments and delusions. She reminds us that all fear is of the mind. If you dare resist, she draws her sword to cut off the stubborn head of your ego, reminding you what really matters in life!

Practice listening to the quiet whispers from Kali who will guide and support you in challenging times.

The notion that She is the goddess of death, sex and violence is also untrue. Kali is the goddess of enlightenment or liberation. Sexuality and mother Kali are not the way of Kali, she is one of the few Goddesses who is celibate practicing austerity and renunciation.

She is portrayed as fierce with gnashing fangs, a protruding tongue, dishevelled hair, dripping blood, a garland of skulls, and a belt of severed arms. Kali represents massive transformation, non-conformity, boundary-pushing, life and death cycles, responsibility and accountability for mistakes, karmic mess clean-up, she's wild and Kali is the essence of freedom and is the force within that transforms fear and sets you free.

Let's remember that death simply represents a transformation into a different form, that's why Kali is often depicted dancing the dance of death.

Kali destroys only what needs to be destroyed - be it a powerful demon, sin, fear or ignorance. Once it's all destroyed, the new creation can begin. So, Kali is the goddess of creation as much as she is the goddess of destruction.

Kali is the consort of the Lord Shiva. It is believed that Shiva is the destroyer; Kali is the Shakti energy which Shiva destroys. Without Kali Shiva would be powerless. And if the entire world ceased to exist, Kali would remain, timeless, formless, similar to a black hole in space.

Kali will help you to become aware of your shadow side. (I talk more about the shadow side in the next chapter.) These are the parts of us that we have hidden from the world because we hold shame, blame and denial around them. The shadow aspects cause us to repress our true emotions, and we can become highly judgemental of ourselves.

To defend this part of ourselves (which we don't want to acknowledge), we project outwardly onto other people. Those parts of ourselves that we find unlovable store trapped energies that would otherwise be flowing freely around the body. So, at the time of trauma, for example being told off in front of the whole school, we don't get a chance to really feel the emotion (Emotion = Energy in motion) the energy gets stuck in the body at the time of the event. This has huge impact on our life force energy.

The Shadow is what we call these places where the darkness is. The places where we carry guilt, shame and denial. To integrate the dark with the light we must have the courage to go into the darkness. Remember that there is no light without darkness. In fact, the darker the night, the brighter the stars. The more we are willing to go into our darkness or 'shadow' the brighter and more joy is experienced on the other side. That's how it works. To become whole again we need to meet our shadow.

Kali will take us with fierce love, to our deepest wounds in order to truly heal them!

Fear is our worst enemy, and remember my beloved sister that you can call upon Kali anytime that you need courage to help you face and transform your fears. You can also call on Kali to support you in working with and getting to know your shadow. Try repeating her name when you need her support and she will give you the strength to believe in yourself and end the illusion of fear.

Om

Kali

Ma!

You are good enough, worthy enough and amazing enough!

Chapter 19
The Goddess Archetypes

In the following chapter we are going to look at the main four Goddess archetypes.

But first, what is an archetype?

The psychologist, Carl Gustav Jung, used the concept of archetype in his theory of the human psyche. Archetypes are images and thoughts which have universal meanings across cultures which may show up in dreams, literature, art or religion.

Jung believes symbols from different cultures are often very similar because they have emerged from archetypes shared by the whole of humanity. He says that our primitive past becomes the basis of the human psyche, influencing our current behaviour. Here are four of the main archetypes that he discovered.

The "persona" or personality (or mask) is the face we present to the world. It is not the real self and Jung describes it as the "conformity" archetype. We have one mask for work, one for being with our friends, and another with our families. We wear so many masks throughout our day that we often no longer know who we really are.

The "anima/animus" The anima is a feminine image in the male psyche, and the animus is a male image in the female psyche. The anima/animus represents the "true self" rather than the image we present to others and serves as the primary source of communication with the collective unconscious.

Each sex manifests attitudes and behaviour of the other simply by centuries of living together. The psyche of a woman contains masculine aspects and the psyche of a man contains feminine aspects.

The combined anima and animus is known as the divine couple. Representing completion, unification, and wholeness.

Next is the "shadow". It is the source of both our creative and destructive side, the unknown "dark side" of our personality, human emotions and impulses like shame, power, selfishness, sexual power, greed, envy, anger or rage. Whatever we deem evil, inferior or unacceptable and deny in ourselves becomes part of the shadow. Projection is how most people deny their shadow, unconsciously casting it onto others to avoid confronting it in oneself.

For example, If I see you as being 'a show off' and it bothers me in any way, then I must own this for myself. The reason that I am agitated and noticing this in you is because there is a part of me that longs to be like you. Very often we have driven this longing so deeply into our subconscious that we are completely unaware of its existence. And then it shows itself as 'projection'.

We project that which we've not owned as our own onto those closest to us. We see them as bossy, mean, selfish, sexual, and repressed. To heal we must be able to say, ' just like me' at the end of any statement.

What we see in others we only notice because it is within us as the shadow. Once we bring up our shadow to the light, by claiming it, owning it, talking about it, honouring it as an experience, then it comes out of the darkness and loneliness and into the light of awareness. We heal not just ourselves but also the collective. It's a win, win.

The last of the main archetypes is the self which is the true self, living without the need for the mask and connecting with the deeper sense of a more spiritual, wiser aspect of self. The self represents the unified unconsciousness and consciousness of an individual. Jung stresses the importance of the True Self archetype because he believed that the goal of human existence is "self-realisation." Self-realisation, as described by Jung, is the "advanced, enlightened psychological state." The awakened being, higher consciousness, or as we often recognise now as fifth dimensional.

We are moving from the 3D world of money, power, control, borders, to a more open hearted and loving 5D world.

It's happening.

So, for Jung the ultimate aim of every individual is to achieve a state of self. He said that the patriarchal culture of Western civilisation has led to the complete devaluation of feminine qualities and the predominance of the persona (the mask) has caused insincerity to a way of life which goes unquestioned by millions in their everyday life.

So that gives you an idea of archetypes, right? SiStar, if you truly want to shine the light of your inner Goddess, learn about these various aspects of your personality and embrace each one fully.

It is now time to invite each of the Goddess archetypes into your life, and love and cherish them deeply!

In each segment below, I will share with you some of the best-known goddesses from various ages and times. By allowing the ancient goddesses to become role models you can really start to develop self-love and appreciation for yourself as the beautiful, wild, free woman that resides within you. Understanding each of the archetypes can help you to come into your power and allow more of your true nature to be loved and witnessed without judgement, fear or resentment.

At the end of each segment I invite you to put down this book and spend a few minutes contemplating the words...... then pick up your Playbook and write whatever comes to mind. For example, you may read the words 'this Goddess makes sure that she takes care of herself....' and then write down your thoughts, fears, concerns, and beliefs around the subject. Or indeed anything that comes to mind. This can lead to great insight and awareness of your programmed ideas and beliefs. Try to notice also any judgements 'popping up' about what you write. You may remember stories from your past or have visions for your future. Whatever comes up for you will be exactly what's meant to be coming up.

I imagine that it might also be interesting to repeat these exercises six months later to see how much you have grown! It is important to remember that 'realizations' are an integral part of spiritual growth. The Goddess awakening to her own power starts to experience deeply nourishing inner peace and contentment! Notice the rate at which you are having these daily realizations, or what I call 'mini awakenings'. When you begin to have them daily, then you'll know that you're in your flow and connected to your Shakti wisdom.

Please be aware that the Goddess is an archetype in her own right and she embodies everything that has already mentioned in this book so far! But she too, has a shadow side. These can manifest as extreme self-indulgence and vanity.

Can you name some of the qualities of the Goddess? And how about her shadow? Can you ask for courage to own her shadow? Can you invite her out of the darkness and into the light to be integrated? Can you do so without judgement, fear, anger? Can you love her? Can you forgive her? Can you see finally that she did everything that she did in order to protect you? She wanted to make you feel so much better. She wanted that for you!

The Warrior Goddess

The Warrior Goddess is a natural leader. She is willing to stand up for her rights and the rights of others who look to her for support and inspiration. She sees her obstacles as challenges, and she's always up for the challenge! She doesn't follow the crowd but her own inner knowing and guidance. This intuitive gut instinct has got better as she has matured in years and experienced life in all its forms. This Goddess is very much in tune with her physical body more than other archetypes, although being embodied is essential if you are to discover the Goddess within (and hopefully by now sister you are already engaging in some form of embodied practice such as dance, yoga, Pilates or simply walking in nature). For this Goddess is also deeply connected with Mother Earth and humanity. She is a Goddess of inspiration and carries with her an energy of quiet poise and calm where she can deal with anything that arises.

Can you claim her?

From my earliest memories I was the oldest sibling, and the one who had to be in charge and organize, defend and take care of my younger siblings. I longed to be the little one (being tall was a major issue for me) the cute one, the irresponsible one.

Losing Steve when I was just 25 years somehow gave me the permission to fall apart in every sense. And yet, because I had two babies I was told 'what a strong woman you are!' No! Now I look back I can say hand on heart that I had to be strong. IT made me strong, although I felt so weak. I survived it. I might have used cigarettes, alcohol, marijuana- but thirty years down the line, I can see now how it shaped me so profoundly! Yours may or may not be quite so dramatic.

What have YOU come through? What did you survive, and how can you allow that warrior archetype to be acknowledged and truly witnessed? I've spent many periods in my life feeling empty, alone, ugly and stuffed down those feelings with smoking and negative self-talk. The warrior in me has taken on her magical powers and pursuits such as listening to motivational speakers whilst walking in the woods and has shifted me energetically into those realms that I speak of when I speak of the Goddess. I've also noticed that I connect quite profoundly to my 'inner warrior' when I dance to tribal music. She takes over, and I am in awe of her. She is amazing!

What triggers you about what I've written? What can you learn about yourself and how can you implement change NOW? How does that make you feel?

The words that come to mind are;

Self-belief, determination, enthusiasm, releasing all doubt, mindfulness, leadership, authentic communication, self-love, power and physical strength.

What words come to mind for you?

The Muses

The Muses were nine beautiful young women who were the goddesses considered to be the personification of knowledge and the arts especially Dance, Literature and Music who remembered all things that had come to pass. They were the nine daughters of Zeus (king of the gods) and Mnemosyne (the goddess of memory). Sometimes they are referred to as water nymphs having been born from the four scared springs on Helicon which flowed from the ground after Pegasus, the winged horse, stamped his hooves on the ground. It was felt that the inspiration of the Muses would help people succeed and prosper. Some of the modern words associated with the Muses are amuse, museum, musing and music.

The Muse is here to support you to live your purpose through your own unique creative expression! She relishes beauty, embodies grace and attracts both effortlessly into her life.

No longer can your innate deepest shakti expression be ignored! She is so ready and now is the time to crack open and finally become who you really are!

Breathe into your dreams, let your inspirations run wild and allow others who touch you to deeply inspire you too for these people are your tribe!

We have reached a new time in our evolution where co creating is the only way forward. Call on your muse Goddess to help you in co creating your dreams and passions and ask her for guidance, love and support!

Can you claim her?

I've always known that I was a dancer. I believe that there is a dancer in each of us. Sure, some people are born gifted, and that includes being gifted the 'right' body in order to 'succeed' commercially. But I'm not speaking of such cultural conditioning as this. When we become embodied in any of the arts, then we become a full expression of the energy that moves through us, and something amazing happens!

For me, that is in dance. For others it is in art, or drama. Self-expression was exciting in the mid-seventies, with the evolution of Punk, and all that it stood for! But sadly, I didn't have the self confidence in myself or in my body. And neither did I want to commit to being labelled in a box as my identity. When I met my punk husband in his kilt, his Mohawk and his Doc Martins, I look back and see how limiting it was for him to be contained by that label! I remember Soft Cell and Marc Almond releasing 'Tainted Love' and Steve bless him loved the song to bits, but would not publicly declare this as it wasn't a punk song with angry words! (We were only twenty-one after all!) So, to create and get in touch with our creative juices it seems vital that we must fully believe in ourselves.

Writing this book has also given me an opportunity to put pen to paper (or more recently I've discovered 'fingertip to iPhone'. Yes- it's possible now dear Goddess to write a book from your iPhone!) Creating the time in my life to express all on these pages has been the hugest gift to myself imaginable! It may have taken me four years - but the satisfaction, the self-expression and the longing to touch others with my story, to share openly from my heart, and to research a subject that has become a personal fascination - has been the gift of a lifetime!

Can you connect now with your own muse, call her in and ask her how she can most assist you?

The Diva!

This Goddess has the confidence to really bring forth that who she really is, with an assured confidence and self-belief! She is very authentic and real in all that she does, whether she is in the limelight, she'll be shining her very bright star continuously! She always uses her intuition, which is powerful, and she now follows this as her guidance in all that she does. She dislikes superficial people, conversations and activities. The Diva Goddess is all about stepping into your personal power and Goddess Lilith is the dark goddess of the Hebrew faith. The Kabbalah describes her as a seductress but as far back as 4000 BCE in the Sumerian culture she was bringing men from the streets to the temple prostitutes

Today she represents a modern archetype of female sexual empowerment. The seductress and the wild woman who has freedom and independence and refuses to be subordinate. She no longer carries the heavy chains and burdening of demoness but has assumed almost heroin proportions to a modern female audience who is eager to explore the sexual shadow. Women nowadays are done with the Christian model of femininity they have been sold for millennia and are exploring opportunities to express themselves from a new perspective. it is safe once again for women to access the full power and spectrum of their sexuality and to explore the shadow. Hallelujah - We are finally starting to heal the wounded feminine.

Can you claim her?

I always remember feeling like I 'd never had much notice taken of me. (not true, but my perception) When I was sixteen I took a Saturday job in a local supermarket, serving cheese, olives and meats from the deli counter. My friend Charlotte also worked there. She had some problems at home, her parents were divorcing, her sister was unstable, and Charlotte was taking time off, crying at work (when she bothered to turn up) and making a big fuss about how she felt. Something clicked in me and in one single moment I learnt that in order to get full attention I need to be 'in crisis'.

Wow!

I didn't know I was going to write that!

That, it would appear, was a vow that I made.

To get attention, I need to be 'in crisis'.

Not too many years later, after being' kicked out of home' as I told everyone, aged nineteen. I had another aha moment that would change the course of my early adulthood.

A younger wayward friend who was hanging out at my new bedsit (yes, I suddenly got very popular getting kicked out of home) stated proudly and defiantly 'I don't give a Fuck about anything!' Woah. I thought.... I'll take that!'

So, looking back, I am noticing that the more I was allowing myself to go into all those defensive modes, the isolation, the abandonment, the low self-esteem, the shame of my body, all those places that stopped me feeling my joy, my true nature- the more I have been able to clearly experience the very contrast. The polar opposite. The light.

I also always despised the small talk that seemed to accompany going out so I'd often find myself sitting in pubs where conversation took precedent over toppling over high heels in a bar. I was shocked a few years ago when I attended a reunion disco, lots of locals from where I lived showed up forty years on, and I danced with a gorgeous fit, strong, handsome man! I thought that my luck was in .I thought he was about to ask me for my phone number, but instead he told me that his wife was at a funeral that day and hadn't felt up to coming out. I heard myself saying 'typical' and as I walked away a few minutes later he whispered in my ear 'you were the girl that all the boys fancied but were too shy to ask you for a dance'.

In that moment I remembered so much. I remembered how I held myself, how beautifully I danced, and how no man ever approached me. I was absolutely useless at being a diva! I hated chat ups, I had no real self-confidence when it came to dating. It all felt fake. My turn on was depth and I never found it at Billy's or Le Beetroot club in London's Soho in the west end. So instead I got drunk and tried to fit in the best I could.

What triggers, or aha moments come to mind for you? Don't hunt for memories, rather allow them to literally 'pop' to mind. These are the ones that hold their gifts for you. You are diving deep inside and I am here to hold your hand, but only should you need it. Take in a deep breath if something painful comes up for you. Shadow work is not easy. Breath, and remember that you are deeply loved, sister.

After the death of my first husband I had a new realization. 'Life is short, don't waste it! 'and 'make it happen!'

I believe now that those earlier experiences showed me contrast, and gave me even more drive to live my life to the full and with full expression of my authentic nature.

Or at least that's how it feels......

Making my dreams become a reality.

It's not about the person you'll become.

It's about the person you are creating.

I'd just like to add here that my beloved mother was going through a difficult time when she screamed at me to leave home when I was nineteen. She loved me very much but could no longer cope and I fully respect that. I had the most amazing and loving mum and for that I shall always be grateful.

The Primordial Mother

There is nothing like the unconditional love of a mother's love. This goddess represents all of nature, motherhood, nurturing, patience, fertility, creation, destruction. When equated with the Earth or the natural world, such goddesses are sometimes referred to as Mother Earth or as the Earth Mother.

Many different goddesses have represented motherhood in one way or another, and some have been associated with the birth of humanity along with the universe and everything in it. Others have represented the fertility of the earth.

The primordial mother embodies love, compassion and trust. She understands the two-way nature of giving and receiving so for that reason she will shower love upon others if and only if, she is able to receive that unconditional love for herself. The primordial mother knows that self-respect is equal to the respect of those whom she loves. She is full of self-love and self-appreciation. Her heart is wide open for she is pure love.

A good mother will provide for her children and always put their needs before her own. You don't need to be a biological mother either- just have the qualities of the nurturer/caregiver.

There is also a shadow side to the mother archetype. The shadow will smother and be fiercely overprotective, or simply have no time to give to her children, in some cases even abandoning them. The shadow can also make her older offspring feel guilty about becoming independent and leaving her 'all alone'

Can you claim her?

When I became a mother as I turned twenty-two, my biological needs were met, and I embraced motherhood and breast-feeding like a duck to water. Although married life to an addict was tremendously challenging, I was massively aware of my Earth Goddess (although of course in those days there was no word other than being a 'hippy mum'.) After Steve died, I became hugely overprotective towards my boys. I would never let them play outside in the street, and my fear of losing the boys, or more aptly it was a fear of someone taking them, was so huge that it pained me to even think about letting them out of my sight for one moment. I became hugely over protective, and would worry myself sick at night in case anything ever 'happened' to them.

Do you connect with your inner mother? Do you hold guilt or shame? Regret? I've noticed how some of my peer group now in their mid-fifties are discovering feelings of regret around choosing to not have children. If you weren't able to have children and wanted to, have you come to terms with that? If you'd had children but struggled with bonding or pain around the experience, how have you integrated? How fully do you appreciate Mother Earth?

Natural Healing Goddess

The natural healing Goddess shares her insights with a gentle authority and precision. She is able to seek and accept help, ask for abundance for her highest good, and make her point without aggression. She understands that her expressions manifest in exactly the way she describes. When she speaks, others hear her, and she is also a great connecter because she understands people. She is often clairaudient in that she senses or hears Angels and other spiritual beings. Call on one of the many goddesses who rule over self-expression and healing: the Irish queen Dana, the butterfly goddess Hina, Hindu goddess of prosperity Sri Laxmi, or the Welsh goddess Rhiannon. She will assist you in using your words wisely!

Can you claim her?

I can claim the connector, I understand others, too much it feels like sometimes. I've learnt from my *Heart IQ* training that I have an ability to actually pick up others' nervous systems! I can express emotions for another who is unable to express repressed emotions through blocks and fears. I have also learnt that it's ok to ask for help when required. Just because you are a mother, a caregiver, a good friend, a good wife, a good sister, does not mean that you cannot ask for help!

Sisters are here for each other!

Sacred Sage

This is the Goddess of self-reflection. These Goddesses teach us to trust our innate wisdom and to allow that wisdom to inspire and guide is in all that we do.

Yes, beloved siStar, this Goddess has got over the 'small stuff' and her life is all about seeing the 'bigger picture'. She knows what is right for her and will no longer be doing with self-judgement and self-criticism. She regularly declutters her life, both physically and mentally, and enjoys the freedom of living simply with minimal fuss and 'stuff' around her.

The Egyptian goddess Isis, the Celtic goddess Brigid and the wise woman, Hecat.

Call on her if you're ready to enjoy daily realizations, mini awakenings, a deeper sense of self, and awaken to the miracles of life happening every single day!

Can you claim her?

I've always been a dreamer, a contemplator and in awe of continual mini awakenings. Life has been one miracle after another, interspersed with so many stories and challenges! Without my sacred sage I'd have never survived. She has kept me from falling into the deepest depression and supported me on my journey more than any other.

High Priestess

The High Priestess of Avalon is the well of Divine Feminine wisdom within us. She is our connection to the esoteric, to the mystery and the magic of the universe. She is healer, she is mother, she is lover. You can call upon your inner priestess through ceremony and ritual. Visit a forest, a lake, a river, sit under the stars and the moon, walk barefoot and raise your palms up towards the heavens. Connect with her through silent contemplation, lighting candles and beautiful sacred music. Through dance, crystals or spirit animals.

The high priestess is a sacred vessel for divine expression. She knows intuitively that she must take time out to connect with her mystical abilities of time travel and has cultivated her gifts of intuition, wisdom, spiritual knowledge. She has absolute clarity about her calling in this lifetime and has done her life 'apprenticeship'. It hasn't been the easiest of journeys, but she shows willing and commitment to the path of self-realisation. She is devoted to this lifestyle and is unable to return to a 'normal' everyday existence. She literally gets 'high' through ritual and sharing her gifts through practices to empower others. She adores meditating, whether it be quietly in front of her alter or simply walking barefoot in nature. She is your connection to Spirit, Universe, God/dess, and the Angels.

Can you claim her?

Hell Yeah!!

I believe that the more we can understand ourselves and who we are, the more love and appreciation we can give ourselves. Only at this point can we genuinely empathise with others. It is true, we can only give love to another to the degree that we can love ourselves.

The Goddess of Love

Meet Goddess Lakshmi, who, of all the Goddesses in the yoga tradition, Lakshmi, the Goddess of love, is perhaps the most sought-after throughout the world. She is called upon for harmony in relationships, wealth, beauty, power, fame, royalty, recognition, and regal grace. That is what LAKSHMI is known for - and yet she is so much more. She is the divine inner spark, the radiant power of grace, and the magnificent sea of abundance within every single person. One of the most concise ways to describe Lakshmi is in Sanskrit: bhukti-mukti pradayini, or "she who bestows both worldly success and spiritual liberation."

A key teaching of Lakshmi is to open to love. She reminds you that the core of the Self is a magnetic power of radiance. She beckons you to stop looking at the surface of life to see your beauty. She cries out to you to stop comparing yourself to each other in a negative way or judging your beauty based on what you see in the magazines and television. She asks that you go inside and truly see the magic within.

Invoke Lakshmi when you can't remember your inner abundance or your true beauty. According to Hindu myth, Lakshmi is born out of the churning of the ocean, seated on a blossoming lotus and surrounded with honeybees and the most fragrant flowers. She is the inner sanctuary within you for every situation in life.

Rhiannon is another Great Goddess of Love. She whispers the language of truth and beauty. She asks us to remember who we are- Sacred Embodiments of Her. We are erotic, sensual, powerful, alive, conscious, compassionate, beautiful, wild, wise and loving, Priestesses of Her Temple which is our body, our mind and our heart.

The Greek goddess of love, Aphrodite, (you've seen the images-of her wearing a simple string of pearls and a couple of scallop shells) reminds us of the transformative powers of sexuality.

You can call upon these very powerful Goddesses at any time - but be warned...her power can turn you into a sexual goddess!

Take your Playbook

Read the above paragraphs about the great goddesses. Allow yourself some quiet time, take in a few deep breaths and close your eyes. Allow each sentence to evoke a loving memory, an insight or a time in your life where you needed support.

Write down your experience and any mini awakenings that you may have.

Goddess of Love, remind me that I don't have to have a partner to be in love, that I can be happy in love with life itself.

Priestess

"The light of the sacred prostitute penetrates to the heart of this darkness.... She is the consecrated priestess, in the temple, spiritually receptive to the feminine power flowing through her from the

Goddess, and at the same time joyously aware of the beauty and passion in her human body."

~ Marion Woodman

Prostitution has often been described as the world's oldest profession transpiring throughout history in all societies. But early forms of prostitution were referred to as "sacred prostitution."

Temples were occupied by Sacred Prostitutes who were also known as Priestesses.

The practice of sacred sex was thought to strengthen the land. "Desire and sexual response experienced as a regenerative power, were recognized as a gift or a blessing from the divine.

Both a man's and woman's sexual nature together with their religious attitude were inseparable.

From this perspective it's not difficult to understand why the practice of sacred prostitution became a religious act of worship where sexuality and spirituality are one and the same.

The temples of the goddess provided for the sacred prostitute far more than is known in this millennium.

The Sacred Prostitute was the original sexual healer.

She was a Priestess, who embodied power, wisdom, purity, and willingness to love with her entire body and soul. These women embodied love and were held in the highest spiritual authority.

They empowered men to reconnect with themselves and spiritual forces through pleasure and prayer.

The Sacred Prostitute was not shamed, viewed as a victim, or "forced into prostitution." She willingly acted from an empowered place of service.

A common practice that took place was called "Taking the War out of a Man." Upon returning from war, men were invited to pass through the Temple doors.

The Priestess would bathe, soothe and knead their physical, emotional and spiritual wounds.

She would expand her magnetic field to absorb all his wounded energy, literally drawing the effects of war from his body, mind and soul.

Through the power of her energy, and purity of her femininity, she would gently and tenderly love him back to wholeness.

Nowadays, the taking the war out of man is more a mental war than a physical war. Men are confused and don't know how to be in this world.

In Ancient times, the sacred prostitute or temple priestess was associated with the religions of the Great Mother Goddess.

My friend Anaiya Sophia and her husband Pete Wilson are offering revolutionary workshops in this area. I believe their work to be at the forefront of a new paradigm where the new language of love is of the highest order.

I met a beautiful young woman in Bali who was on a sacred journey and was offering naked Lingham massage. She had this to say

"As you know I plunged deeply into the Tantric community, investing quite a fair bit of resources to learn some powerful and painful lessons. It was an insight into spiritual narcissism and some dark themes in the world, their existence in me and also influence in keeping me small and powerless.

It certainly does not falter at the Tantric doorstep, it is prevalent in the psyches of those in high power roles in the wider non-spiritual community. Dark energy that I am no longer afraid to speak of. It seems that the sacredness and allure of our past lives, past energetic

awareness has lost a part of the holiness, healing, sanctity, appreciation and reverence. It has become adulterated, egoist, misconstrued and misunderstood. It has become unwarranted and delusional. Sexuality and intimacy has become warped and tainted. It is different to the sacred prostitute of ancient times. I have loved and felt deeply for the energy of the sacred whore.... running the energy of Inanna, Magdalene....attempting to bring this light energy into the work and have returned broken hearted to the cold hard truth that there are many who do not want awareness, who do not want to take responsibility for their energy, who do not want to inhabit their body as a sovereign compassionate being, feel empathy for another....be truly human.

The Sacred Prostitute was never about women selling their bodies to please and serve men to their detriment".

We need to look beyond these kinds of self-destructive behaviours.

The prostitute is a metaphor for the kind of healing that happens when we give ourselves over to love and to the possibility of allowing joy to happen throughout our bodies and in our lives.

We grow by expanding from old boundaries into a new awareness. This is the place from which we grow. First, we must learn to love and please ourselves, then we can learn to love and please others. That is the true sacredness.

Take your Playbook

Take some time to write the story of your sexual journey in this life. Once you complete that, think about whether you would be willing to share this with those close to you. Explore the possibility that by taking this vital aspect of yourself out of the shadows and into the light, you can bring more acceptance.

Shaman and the Goddess

'Woman is by nature a shaman'

~ Chukchee Proverb

Geoffrey Ashe, a noted British scholar of shamanism, wrote that shamans were originally women, and that the oldest form of the word "shaman" refers to "female shaman." He says that ancient shamanism was not an individual phenomenon but something that was practiced by the female group. And the power of the female group is biologically rooted in menstruation and the blood mysteries of birth

A shaman is one who flies between the worlds, and who has a foot in both worlds — that of the seen and unseen. When a woman bleeds, she enters the world of the unseen, the world of dreams, intuition and spirits. Because we, in the west, are not educated in these ancient ways of seeing, we do not know how to embrace them. But, with Goddess re-emerging, our memories are returning, and we are remembering.

In matriarchal days gone by, women would bleed together in rhythm with the moon, and this was seen as a primal shamanic art. Giving birth, and all its messiness are the gift of the Earth–elemental chaos coming into form.

Honouring mothers as the first shamans honours all of us. Recognizing that without our mother's love, nurturance, and healing wisdom we would die, and that respecting our mothers teaches us respect for the Great Mother.

It was generally believed that shamans were male. As with so many other faiths, it has been the male that takes on the more 'powerful' role. But with the new uprising in Goddess faiths of recent decades we are now reclaiming our equality! Shamanism is the root of all world religions and spiritual practices. Ancient tribal cultures relied upon their shamans for healing, advice on nature's medicinal herbs and medicines, and to share spiritual knowledge. It was in fact the Shamans who developed stories of Gods and Goddesses, and the myths of modern cultures!

Chapter 20
A Love Story

I was exhilarated beyond what I thought was humanly possible after returning home from the Netherlands and my first Heart IQ retreat. It was a seven-day retreat and part of my year-long Heart IQ facilitator training. It was liberating, and it was my first experience of meeting in circle and relating at the deepest level with other human beings willing to have their hearts cracked open. I'd been on several weekends with some beautiful people and also some who'd triggered me enough for me not to want to return. I'd actually walked out on two different 'circle' facilitator trainings until I found the one that resonated. It's something I guess I've always been; fussy, and very aware of if something 'fits' or not.

Prior to leaving for the retreat, which I'd been looking forward to for so long, my dear soul sister Rachel was just starting to come out of a ten-month period of depression. I'd only met Rachel eighteen months earlier, and although we'd known of each other for over thirty years, we hadn't connected like we did after Rachel asked to meet me in Bali. So, I'd never really known about her long challenges with mental health. What I saw was a funny, beautiful, caring, kind, sexy, vulnerable Goddess!

It was May 2014 and Rachel arrived just in time for what we discovered was going to be a joint birthday celebration- May 7th would be my 53rd birthday and Rachel's 43rd birthday!

In my entire life I had never experienced a soul sister meeting such as this one. Rachel was so similar to me- mannerisms, singing songs (a lot), infectious laughter, playfulness, a love of spontaneous outbursts of dancing anywhere and everywhere - and some very deeply painful and traumatic life experiences.

Rachel's life story however, had been more traumatic than mine. Her mother had died from a brain haemorrhage after years of abuse from her father and Rachel was just fourteen when she lost her mother, having just discovered that she was pregnant. Rachel ran away from home and was then housed by a family who took in the fourteen-year-old mum to be, and was then sexually abused by the man in the house. The story goes on and on.

A particularly poignant moment that I will always remember was one Sunday when we sat together in Starbucks and reminisced how when our children had been younger that Sundays' were so different! When you're single and the kids have grown up, unless you make a point of planning your weekends, then Sundays can sometimes feel quite painfully lonely. It was mother's' day, 2015. I spoke to Rachel about my own beloved mother who had passed eleven years earlier at just 65 years old. It had felt so unbelievably cruel- like the worst loss imaginable. My depth of sorrow for my mother gave Rachel permission and comfort to feel into the loss of her own mother twenty-eight years earlier.

I was shocked when she told me that it was the very first time she had cried over the loss of her mum! I was both humbled and honoured that Rachel had felt safe enough with me to share this profound moment of release after such a long time. I have always been someone whom people confide in, but it's rare in a lifetime I believe to feel such a soulmate connection with another. I would go as far as to say it felt like more than soulmate.

I used to call her 'my little sister' but in fact I thought of her as a young version of myself. Rachel certainly brought out my fun loving crazy side- and she used to say that I was the only person she'd ever met who could be crazier than her! The difference was that I'd never gotten myself addicted to alcohol or cocaine or dangerously destructive and narcissistic relationships. I'd never watched my mother being battered by my father. I'd never been abused nor watched my mother lose her fight for life, whilst pregnant and aged just fourteen, damn it. Just writing it makes me shudder.

A few weeks before attending my Heart IQ retreat, Rachel was surfacing from the depths of severe depression, having not responded to my calls, my visits nor my texts in around six months. Prior to her 'lying low in deep depression' Rachel had recently trained to become a laughter yoga teacher. We would drink green juices and create exotic smoothies, talk about men, love, life and ideas for workshops, places to travel and moan about our adult kids not understanding us! She cooked me amazing meals, we went for Sunday drives in my big old Land Rover and shared our deepest longings. Our birthday together in Bali was the happiest birthday of my entire life (and I've had some good ones!).

Three days before I left for my 7 days retreat in Holland I told Rachel that I was so happy that she was coming out of her depression and she asked me how long I was going away for. She'd got herself back into a 'bad crowd' and without my knowing was also spending time away from the shackles of her room and keeping company with some dark energies who were using her kindness and vulnerability for their own empowerment.

Rachel told me that she wanted to slowly start doing some 'normal' things again, like dog walking together, which we'd spent hours upon hours doing after returning from Bali. She'd even started making her green juices and was hoping to rid this depression again like she'd done so many times before. But she said to me that our time together had been the happiest days of her life. *That felt so incredibly special.*

I saw Rachel the night before I left for the airport and I told Rachel that I would be back in seven days. She seemed upset that I was leaving so soon after she was ready to start gently easing back into socialising again.

Fast forward a week and I had the best week ever! Connections were made like I've never experienced before in my life and processes rolled one after the other. Tears of grief, pain, joy all simultaneously merging into one heart softening, vulnerability awakening journey to self.

My Heart IQ experience was everything I'd wanted it to be!

I returned home exhausted and exhilarated, and couldn't wait to tell Rachel how much she could benefit from the *heart circling* events that I was now holding regularly. She had so enjoyed the women's group that I'd created, in fact it was one of the most profoundly life changing (literally) groups that any of us in the circle had ever experienced!

So, the very next morning I went around to Rachel's house and knocked on the door. I knocked so many times over the past ten months to be met by silence, wondering where she was, who she was with and if she was simply sleeping. I had a house key and several times had asked a friend to accompany me for fear of what I might find.

There was an eeriness about the place. The bedroom curtains were closed as they often were. I wanted to share with my soul sister what had happened during my powerful retreat. And I wanted us to hang out again, like we'd done before her depression had got hold of her again.

The next morning, I had a phone call. It was the worst news imaginable.

'Rachel is dead'

I threw the phone towards a friend who'd popped by and collapsed trembling in disbelief. The words wouldn't/couldn't go in. I stood up and walked around and around the room, up the stairs and back again. My friend spoke with the friend who'd called. I just couldn't take it in. It was too big. The two other loves of my life had got sick and then died. The father of my children and my beloved mother. It was devastating in itself. This was something different. I didn't expect it. It'd crossed my mind a few times, but I didn't believe it would ever actually happen. I was numbed, traumatized and in total shock!

It was one week before 'our' birthday and Rachel was just 44 years old. Her son had found her in bed, that poor boy. Her body had been there for at least three days, and so she'd been there in her room the night I knocked and called out her name.

I was beyond devastated, it seemed cruel, unfair and unimaginable.

Fast forward two weeks and I was co-hosting my very first circling weekend with a beautiful couple I'd met through the circling community. They were not trained with Christian Pankhurst, nor Tej Steiner, both of whom I'd studied with, but another organization called circling Europe. They travelled a long way to get to me, as did a few other co facilitators, one flying in from the Netherlands. It was going to be an exciting event!

Circling is all about being radically honest, authentic and real. I was still in deep shock over Rachel's death. It is absolutely against all agreements to share anything of our sacred time in circle. But what I want to share is this, and this is allowed.

I allowed the part of me that felt abandoned, crazy, wild, grief-stricken, shocked to be witnessed I also welcomed in the part of me that was trying to hold myself together, the part of me that nearly cancelled the event, the huge empty hole in my heart, the vulnerable little girl who was experiencing loss again. Once she had made herself known, she took on the role of facilitator the way that she knew how to. The 'problem' was that she triggered a few other people present in the circle. This is very 'normal' in circle.

As in circle as in life.

By the end of the powerful weekend so much had happened, this again, is usual and expected. But what distressed me was how one of my co facilitators had left the circle several times throughout the weekend to be alone. When I spoke with her partner months later I was told that I had triggered her. I felt 'wrong' I really don't like to trigger people and, yet I do it a lot it seems in circle.

I too had been triggered. The couple had left at the end of the weekend without helping me to clear up. I was in fact so triggered that I burst into tears as my old story of 'I am not supported' was playing out perfectly! Lucky for me there were a few big strong men there to give me a hug and an ear. That's not usually the case and I was so grateful for some moral support in tidying up and clearing the space (physically and energetically) in my studio.

I attempted to make contact with my beautiful co facilitator months after the event, but she was now pregnant and in full flow and I really didn't want to bring up any old grievances.

Forward to Feb 2017 and I've had a message asking if I'd like to co facilitate again. I felt that I really wanted to reach out to my friend whom I had triggered. I wanted to understand exactly what had happened. I cannot approach anything with any unfinished uncleared blocks. We arranged a time to skype and the conversation we had last night felt like it drew a line under all the pain from last year.

I want to add that the lady in question is a young and very conscious and beautiful woman. I held her in high esteem for her incredible wisdom at such a young earthly age.

It turned out that on the weekend she had just found out that she was pregnant. They had both wanted to keep it a secret for fear of a threatened miscarriage: in fact, she had been warned that this could be likely. She was triggered by my strength and my power.

Personally, I was ashamed of how I'd behaved (at times) on that weekend, because my emotions were running so wild. But I could now empathise with her, because her emotions were also running wild! She was in fact protecting herself and her unborn child. As we spoke, I felt deeply stirred in my womb and the tears began to flow. Not from sadness but from pure and exquisite joy. I was again experiencing the kind of connection that we had enjoyed on earlier weekends and before we had co facilitated the weekend last year.

Although I had spoken to her partner since the weekend, who was also a facilitator, I hadn't had any idea whatsoever of their personal situation. I felt enormous waves of love and peace and compassion fill my body. I spoke softly, and I felt tender, quiet and raw. Tears streamed. My voice mimicked hers, soft, gentle and feminine. I noticed triggers of my own, young families being together. I never had that. I had wanted it so badly that it hurt to my core. I noticed the trigger rise and then subside. I noticed myself enjoying the energy of fragility, tranquillity and vulnerability and most of all I felt hugely humbled.

I want to tell you something, I said to my friend....

'I LOVE You!'

When we speak from the depths of our soul there is a benevolence, and it may not always appear to show as and when we want it to. Human beings are so complex. But we always attract people, situations and experiences that come to us for one reason only: to know ourselves more.

Love stories are all around us.

Take your Playbook and write a love story. It might be the story of your meeting your partner, of losing a close friend, of being in awe of your beautiful grandchild or Godchild. It can be anything that you want it to be.

If you knew just how magnificent and beautiful you were, you would literally fall at your own feet.

Chapter 21
We are all Witches

At a recent heart circling weekend event one of the male facilitators declared to a female participant (during a highly passionate energy exchange of words) 'You are just a witch!' to which my friend responded 'You'd better believe it!' as she stood tall (all 5 foot of her) and warrior like. My friend Jenny is starting to truly embody her sacred powers, her warrior womanhood and her Shakti! When I first met Jenny she had been attending the annual Goddess conference in Glastonbury, England, for many years. I have watched Jenny transform over the past few years since attending my weekly Heart Circling meetings and following the path of awakening through listening to spiritual teachers via YouTube and attending workshops and seminars. She is truly open to growth and becoming more of her true self. It is becoming less rare that I meet other women like myself who are willing to really put spiritual growth at the top of their priorities... and to see the results is so satisfying, beautiful and inspiring. However too many of my sisters are still denying the full expression of their true self, and much of this I put down to what happened to us as wise women all those thousands of years ago.

Jenny said that after her experience with this guy (a friend and fellow Heart Circling participant) that during the tea break she literally went and sat in her car and howled! The interaction had literally erupted, as all of her powerful sacred repressed Goddess witch energy was being downtrodden and shouted down right there for us all to witness!

And this wise woman was conscious enough to feel into her own innate truth and powerfully respond from her core! Jenny's voice in that moment became a cry from the collective. The woman in each of our sisters, mothers, and grandmothers who has been lost in the abyss, feeding from the fallout of repression and violation.

I love how Jenny calls herself a witch. Being a witch is all about intuition. But sadly the word witch has been steeped in shame and cast into the shadow. And I do not blame men either because it is not their fault.

This short chapter is written to inform you siStar that we are all witches!

And when we connect to our true innate beautiful feminine Goddess, priestess, sacred woman energies- then our inner witch can literally appear in all of her glory!

Witchcraft was literally just that - a craft. The word witch used to mean 'wise woman' and all the priests were against it. Thousands of women were burned in Europe in the Middle Ages because the priests could not understand the world of intuition. They only knew 'intellect'. To them it looked dangerous and strange and they didn't understand it so they decided to destroy it! They literally wiped out one of the most beautiful qualities of the feminine, of receptivity, of a higher knowledge, of realms that were higher states of being other than the mind's perception. And they created such fear that women lost the capacity to keep their deep intuitive powers!

In the middle ages the women who were called witches were burned at the stake. It was not really ever against witchcraft, it was against women. We owe that shadow to patriarchy. SiStars, please remember that patriarchy is not male, not gender, but a perversion of masculine energy which brutalized, raped and suppressed the feminine.

Those women who were burned, killed, murdered, tortured when they showed any sign of having intuitive gifts were thought to be witches. If the man showed the same kind of talent he became worshipped and the woman would become a witch.

She was cast into the hands of the devil and the man was a gift from god.

The word `witch' is actually a beautiful word. It means a wise woman; there is nothing wrong in it. But these wise women were dangerous to the priests, who could not allow any competitors; hence the very word `witch' became derogatory. They must have burned thousands of beautiful women, forced them to confess that they were witches. And they said that the meaning of witch was that the women were in a sexual relationship with the devil! For many women, to reclaim the word Witch is to reclaim one's self and her relationship to the Great Mother.

Look at history of the enlightened ones. Their whole lives have been intrinsically woven with women who were not approved by society. If we take Magdalene as an example – she was known as the prostitute who was associated with Jesus.

For thousands of years, the Goddess has embodied and endured the collective torment and has been written out of his-story. Verses written by women were removed from sacred books and texts. Never were women granted a voice. Enlightened souls such as Buddha and Jesus were associated with prostitutes but this was just a mask. The movie Mary Magdalene, directed by Garth Davis, is a significant portrayal of this early Christian figure in the light of evidence from the earliest texts. The screenwriters, Helen Edmundson and Philippa Goslett, are quite clear that Mary is not to be associated with Jesus through her sexuality, or a wife as has always been the case so far in his-story... Mary Magdalene was to be depicted as an honest, intuitive and faithful disciple of Jesus.

I suggest that if you've not watched this epic film already that you go and watch it. Mary Magdalene is so beautifully portrayed in the movie. She possesses an incredible and compelling presence, which is not how the later texts portrayed her.

So now you know siStar, I love you and your witchy powers!

Practice them over and over........

"Where there is woman, there is magic."

~ Ntozake Shange

Chapter 22

Conscious Relationships

OK so we've covered prostitution, high priestesses and witches and all sorts of other ways in which society has deemed the Goddess to be 'wrong'!

What are your thoughts so far?

Can you take your Playbook and write down your thoughts and feelings?

I've been writing this book for years now and I keep on reading it. No lie! Every time I start to write a new chapter I start to ponder over the words I've written, and I become mesmerised. The book works! This 'work' works!

But one thing is essential.

You must practice! You must cultivate, tender to and nurture your whole being into presence. As much as possible. Daily. Whenever you can! Turn off your TV, and make room in your life NOW for a new way of being!

This in essence, is a conscious relationship. In fact, you know already what I'm going to say, right? I'm going to tell you that you cannot, simply cannot have a conscious relationship with another until you have one with yourself!

Aaargghh I hated those words. I really didn't 'get' how anyone could be seriously happy inside and out unless they were in a loving relationship!

But guess what? I found the keys to lasting love - and I share them all in my online course, how to meet the love of your life

So, what exactly is a conscious relationship?

In a conscious relationship there's an invitation to feel anything, absolutely nothing needs to be hidden, closed down, denied or resisted.

So, let's start with you! Now with another this can feel quite a difficult thing to do. But it's important to be honest with yourself first. My hope is that by reading this book so far that you've been triggered into some memories, thoughts and ideas.

Put down this book and simply ask yourself 'How do I feel? Visit your physical body, your emotional, your mental and your spiritual bodies. Breath. Listen. I'll do it too, right now

As I write this I am sitting in a 24-hour Starbucks where I live in St Albans. I had got everything sorted, with tenants living in my house helping to pay my mortgage and thus allowing me the freedom to teach less hours (to be honest I'm done with teaching Pilates) I feel so much more than that! So, I just found out that one tenant hasn't been paying his rent. I found out too that he's addicted to cocaine.

I had to rid his room of vodka bottles & beer cans, reminding me of all the years that I did this many years ago, when my boys' rooms were constantly in the most despicable mess. I felt so sad that this lovely bright, 'chirpy chappy' is so broken, so addicted to not feeling, that he has lost everything. His job, his family, his self-worth. He has disappeared, and his family have given up on him. I have his stuff, his new TV, his crockery and his designer hoodies. His kind-hearted sisters have apparently bailed him out 'once too many times' and won't do again. I must decide if I will take his belongings to a charity shop (and not the tip as they suggested) or find a place to store the six or so refuse sacks containing all his worldly possessions. I feel so sad. This young man had reminded me of my own son. Of my own boys who'd had such a difficult start in life... But not just the boys, but also reminds me of my first husband. Not long after Steve died I found an envelope hidden underneath the bath panels (of all places) I was shocked to remember the circumstances that would lead up to finding this envelope.

Adam had been just two years old when Steve was working for British Rail. Every week I would make a list of all the bills that would need paying. Gas, electric, rent, food, cigarettes. The kind of list that you make when times are hard and you're trying to be a grown up and responsible mummy.

One Saturday Steve and I queued up at our local post office to pay the phone bill. Adam started to yell in his pushchair. So, I left Steve in the post office to queue and took my son over the road and into a toy shop that would keep him quiet. I remember always thinking that people would judge us for being bad parents if we looked like punks and had a screaming child in tow.

I could literally feel people's judgements towards us, even though Steve had shaved off his big blue Mohican hairstyle when I'd become pregnant, we still apparently looked 'different' to the majority of residents in middle class suburbia in the early eighties.

A few weeks later my grandparents invited me to spend some time with them at their home in Skegness, a seaside town in Lincolnshire. It was agreed that my beloved grandfather would drive myself and Adam and that Steve would join us for the weekend after finishing his last shift at work.

One night I went to find a phone box (yes this is before the age of mobiles!) and was alarmed to find that I couldn't get through to my husband. I tried again the next morning. After many attempts I called the operator and eventually called BT who told me that I'd had my phone line disconnected. I yelled 'but I saved weeks for my bill payment and we paid your bill a few weeks ago!' I can even remember queueing in the post office!' I insisted that British Telecom make a full enquiry as to why my phone had been cut off in error! I was fuming.

And then it dawned on me in a sudden flash of terror. I'd put the phone bill money in an envelope marked 'phone money' and handed it to Steve in the post office assuming that whilst I took our screaming son to another shop, that he would make it to the counter at the post office and pay the phone bill! When I found the envelope marked 'phone money' behind the panels it all made sense. I had my evidence. Had he wanted me to find out? Why did he leave the proof of his lies for me to find one day?

My husband's addiction to gambling and lying was like a cancer that would destroy my family.

Many years later my son also had a problem with smoking, and spending his money on an addiction. He eventually left his hometown in his late twenties to rid himself of the bind of the dreaded weed community. It's rife in our world today. Too many young people (perhaps 'young can include the under sixties?)! are battling with addictions that are consuming their lives.

What I describe above is one example of my relationship that was not conscious. I was living in fear. Fear is the opposite of truth. Truth is love. I was afraid to be alone. I was afraid to not have a man in my life. So, I attracted what I was most afraid of. I somehow attracted what felt like hell. If I had been conscious I would never have allowed myself to go through that hell. But my soul needed it in order to know the opposite. How can I know heaven if I don't know hell?

Letting go of our suffering is the hardest work we will ever do. It is also the most fruitful. To heal means to meet ourselves in a new way, in the newness of each moment where all is possible, and nothing is limited to the old.

Becoming more authentic is a journey of letting go of identification with knowledge that is not yours in the 1st place. So that means that to know what a conscious relationship is it's no good simply reading about it! We must look at our own relationships, our own lessons and our own triggers.

"If I accept the fact that my relationships are here to make me conscious, instead of happy, then my relationships become a wonderful self-mastery tool that keeps realigning me with my higher purpose for living."

~ Eckhart Tolle

To be in a conscious relationship means to be committed to growth, be it spiritual, mental, physical, or even sexual.

Each person wants the other to reach their full potential and will support them with that. I was shocked just yesterday when a close friend of mine called me and asked if we could meet up.

One of her work colleagues had been given a death sentence after the return of her cancer, and had been transferred to a hospice. She sadly passed over yesterday, and my friend Aly was devastated. I asked her if her friend and colleague had any family. She responded that there was a partner whom she was about to marry and a son in his twenties. I asked her about siblings. Yes, she said 'she has a sister who came down from Wales and whom she hasn't seen for five years! The sister came down to the hospice a few days ago.

'Ah that's so lovely' I said, 'that the sister was with her when she passed'. 'No' said my friend. 'She runs a small business with her husband, and he's very controlling. He insisted she came back home and so Tanya died after her sister was demanded to return home to help her husband in the business.' This woman didn't even get to be with her sister as she passed away because of a controlling husband! It was the reason she'd not seen her sister in five years! This is an example of a non-conscious, very controlling and needy marriage! And I believe that this is more common than you might think. But times are changing. More people are looking for something different because the old way didn't work. There is a new paradigm emerging.

Conscious relating means taking responsibility for your own darkness.

Not blaming it on another and not controlling, bullying, denying or abusing. We must fight our own demons and face our own shit...Oftentimes I see as an outsider, and as a coach, that men and women may know that 'something isn't right' but they try to put the blame on their partner for triggering them. Or they don't have the courage or insight to do anything about the situation.

In the case of my friend's colleague, that sister will never have the chance to buy back the precious time she could've spent with her beloved sister. She may end up blaming her husband. But ultimately, she had a choice in that moment. To 'obey' her husband's command to return home, or to sit with her sister in her final hours. It's often not until a situation becomes unbearable that I get the phone call to step in. And being conscious is about being totally and completely honest, Real, authentic and transparent. You must be ready for truth.

I find that very often one of the couple is fearful that their partner will shut down when the one who is ready for change bares his/ her soul. But we simply, cannot allow that to stop us from being authentic!

All feelings, emotions, and everything that we share, and expose are welcomed into the relationship, because the primary goal is to grow.

And growth is not always comfortable!

When we take responsibility for ourselves, it means that we own our wounds, our conditioning, and every experience we've ever had.

Taking responsibility requires healthy communication so that each person can understand where the other is coming from.

When two people who individually own their shit come together and be open and honest with each other without becoming triggered, then there is the opportunity for real love.

When we are able to dedicate our relationships to the well-being and growth of both ourselves and the other, we begin to experience what it means to love another.

I Love YOU

And remember...

You are beautiful in more ways than you could ever know....

Chapter 23
Rise Shakti!

Feminine power is rising!

I feel it in my bones! In my blood!

My feminine energy is sexual, wild, tender, and vulnerable- and it's waiting for you too!

Dare you stand in your sacred sexual creative energy, walk tall and with pride for being woman and breath life and magic into your dreams?

In December 2016, I attended an ecstatic dance event in Ubud, Bali. I'd somehow managed to ignore my love of dance for too long. I don't know too many over fifties who go to ecstatic dance, but that didn't stop me. I was feeling young and carefree. And I'd lost the extra pounds that'd been sitting around my hips and belly, so was feeling trim and gorgeous. Now, I'm not saying that overweight isn't sexy, because if I'm completely honest, I see sexier radiant large women than I do slim women. But what I am saying is that when I cut down on extra sugar and carbs. I feel lighter energetically, healthier, less bloated, and more capable of gyrating my body to the sound of tribal ecstatic trance! No alcohol. No drugs. Just pure Shakti energy pouring through my veins.

The energy that is raised in ecstatic dance, and also in 5rythms is immense!

You don't need to know how to dance. You need to feel into the energy and allow the music to move you. You are not the dancer, but you are allowing yourself to 'be' danced.

I began to attend these sessions more often, listening to my body when I felt tired and exploding with pure ecstasy and rhythm when my mind fully surrendered to the beat. My natural body rhythm literally began to take over! I got 'out of my head' and felt as if the angels had enveloped me with their big angel wings and transported me to a world where having a body was no longer necessary! The pure waves of ecstasy pulsating through my being were in fact connecting me into a higher dimension. Having a body with senses was helping me to experience this state.

I thought to myself 'isn't this what we all strive for constantly? To feel such freedom and abandonment that I no longer even need to own a body! For my connection to the Almighty is so powerful and strong! This is what I came here to remember!

(Can you feel the wave of orgasmic energy in my words?)

OK I've calmed down now.

A few weeks later and back in the UK, I found a 5rythms class that I'd attended previously once before two years earlier. I knew that this was in my blood. I wanted more.

Without much thought I found myself committing to bring more ritual and sacredness into my daily life. I looked up priestess trainings (again, I'd read up years earlier, but the timing hadn't been right).

As I turned 56 I headed back to Bali to train as an ecstatic dance facilitator. And I signed up to study for 2 years with the Priestess Rhiannon course. The Goddess of love and sacred sexuality.

I am going to be pushed way beyond my comfort zone- I just know it. Watch out Glastonbury, I am heading your way!

What courses and trainings have you ever thought about?

What's crossed your mind?

Which longings/ hobbies/interests/creativities have you pushed aside?

'We have learned to be a little lukewarm with our longing. And if we bring lukewarm to our spiritual practice, lukewarm is what we will get. Your longing is Shakti—pure energy—and arises from the source of your being. Open yourself to that more vulnerable place in your heart, where you make the longing in your heart matter.

From this place, miracles can happen; life can touch you'.

~ Chameli Ardagh

Chapter 24
The Next Chapter

For the past few months I've been trying to ignore the messages of my soul. This is ironic because I've been writing a book for the last four years on how to be a middle-aged Goddess. You know how they say that 'you teach what you most need to learn? Well, I'm writing this book for me, and I so want and know that I can inspire you to do the same!

I'm living in a room which used to be a shed and we had it extended and smartened up. Paul and I used the original 'outhouse' as a recording studio in the early nineties. In those days we were the hippest couple because we owned a four-track recording studio.

Then my ex-partner and I had the small space extended, adding a glass roof and an internal door, separating the area with a wall so that clients from the studio could use the WC in private! Teejay used the space as his office and then as a massage room. I've been so inventive and creative with my home space.

Renting out the rooms in my house, and living simply in one room has enabled me to finally give up teaching Pilates classes. I've had the same clients for decades and I'm ready, although it's been happening so gradually, to finally fly the nest.

When I wake up to the sound of the ocean, something happens to me at a cellular level. I have beautiful siblings here and beautiful friends.

It's a little difficult to listen to the heart when the head is so dominant in its justifications. The favourite story running recently is that 'Liz you're not happy so you're running away. You want a relationship and you're unsettled.' In comes heart. She says 'I adore you. You are a free spirit. You came here to love. To experience. To travel. To be authentic. To be open. To write. To share. To make new friends, to inspire, to create.

She knows!

How does she know?

Ok try this for yourself. Give yourself some options. Don't judge the ideas as 'daft "impossible' or 'unattainable' feel into what you are thinking, pondering, longing, experiencing.

Now for half a minute at a time take yourself into each possible scenario. Notice the reaction in your physical body. Then notice your emotions. Do the same for each idea. Guess which one is the truth of the heart?

Tell me!

Write the experience, including listing the various options, and write about how you feel on each one.

Last week when I spoke with my teacher and told her how I felt like everything was ending, she told me 'Liz, you are having a spiritual awakening'

I'd been feeling restless, in the wrong place, tired of sharing my home with strangers and bored with the same old clients, not all of them by any means, but the few who'd grown to rely on me and yet not want me to grow. The final straw came a few months ago when I started to talk about how the masculine aspect of Pilates was not the whole picture. That we need the feminine flow and chaos and that within that lies the balance of the masculine and feminine. One of my clients said, 'oh Liz I really don't believe in all that!'

And in that moment, I thought 'do you know what - I really don't want to teach you anymore.

I'd thought it many times over the past five years, but this time felt different. I knew that it was the end.

I was now caught up in working purely for an income. A passion of mine has become a chore. Clients who had begrudged my lifestyle and travel had died off and left and the committed ones no longer really wanted to expand and grow. I had become their comfort blanket, their security, their Thursday morning fix. I knew this time that I wanted to sell up and move away.

I thought I'd wanted to keep the same clients forever! And I felt my whole adulthood lodged into the bricks and mortar of my home. Thirty years living in the same place, married, divorced, lovers, children, partners, making love by the fireplace, kissing for hours, old memories, happy, sad, stoned, joy, sorrow.

The words 'spiritual awakening' aroused my ego.

Wahaaay!

But a deeper sense of truth emerged.

I feel that I'm finally getting to know who I really am. Beyond the drama. Beyond the need to control, to be the provider, mum, dad, guru, teacher, healer, ego driven, survival.

Hidden so well by status!

I want to strip myself naked at the altar.

And serve humanity in any way I can offer my gifts.

I hope that you will read this book over and over as I have done, that you will allow yourself to be aroused, on every level and without holding back. I trust that you will have the insight to notice when your inner critic takes hold. That you will call in your inner Goddesses as and when they are needed.

I do it all the time.

You can do that too.

I bow to you.

You are amazing!

You are awesome!

You are the light!

You inspire me with your longings!

You inspire me with your depth, your willingness to grow, and your vulnerability.

And……

Never, ever forget ……

That you are loved beyond measure.

You came here to learn.

You came here to grow.

You came here to get messy, to feel, to laugh, to expand.

And….

I love you, siStar ❤

Every time I feel unsure, lost or disconnected I remind myself that whatever it is that I'm feeling, is experienced by you too. We are so powerfully connected sisters!

The words in this book are intended for you to read and read again and again. Every time I read these words I myself feel as if I've stopped off at the 'spiritual service station'. Ha, I love that description! It's sooooooo apt!

I too need filling up, especially as I take steps towards greater heights of awareness, creativity. Self-belief, inner peace, self-acceptance, joy and healing.

I too have all of the insecurities that you have! But I have practiced the magic in this Playbook book over and over and over. Each time I've done a proof read of these chapters, I am reminded of the powerful messages of absolute possibility and I've watched my life change dramatically from the inside out.

The very moment I take some bold and courageous step towards what my heart longs for I ask my inner goddess for her love, presence & guidance. As I complete this book, in May 2018, I'm aware of how incredibly powerful and transformed I'm feeling on a much deeper level.

I am ready for true love...

Becomes a declaration...

I AM true LOVE

Please be patient. Do the exercises. Ask for support from each of the Goddesses described in this Playbook , and without judgement allow yourself to connect to the beautiful, wise, healthy, sexy, gorgeous, kind, clever, loving, Mother Earth Goddess that you came here to experience .

She is YOU.

Dear Human: You've got it all wrong. You didn't come here to master unconditional love. That is where you came from and where you'll return. You came here to learn personal love. Messy love. Sweaty love. Crazy love. Broken love. Whole love. Infused with divinity. Lived through the grace of stumbling. Demonstrated through the beauty of messing up. Often. You didn't come here to be perfect. You already are. You came here to be gorgeously human. Flawed and fabulous. And then to rise again into remembering. Love doesn't require the condition of perfection. It only asks that you show up. And do your best. That you stay present and feel fully. That you shine and fly and laugh and cry and hurt and heal and fall and get back up and play and work and live and die as YOU.

~ Courtney A. Walsh

Your Notes

* 9 7 8 1 9 1 2 2 4 3 2 5 9 *

#0010 - 230718 - C44 - 210/148/13 - PB - 9781912243259

and ideas but at the same time as you guide me, and support me, and help me. Without you I wouldn't be able to get anywhere, be able to achieve anything, create a business, create the life that I want to create for us. You are my reason for getting up in the mornings. The kids are important and they are to me, but at the same time every morning that I get to wake up with you. I'm blessed, I'm gifted, I'm just so thankful for everything you've ever done. And for all the life that we're going to have together, I'm just so grateful and blessed that you decided you wanted to have that amazing life with me I love you .

Printed in Great Britain
by Amazon

50065111R00112